LIVING
OUT OF
CONTROL

Praise for *Living Out of Control*

In his latest book, the inestimable Rodney Clapp offers a great gift to the Christian community for this moment. With remarkable brevity, drawing on his wide-ranging and eclectic reading interests, and always deeply rooted in the biblical text, Clapp diagnoses a major current Christian problem—a desperate grasp for control—and offers a way to get us to a solution: learning to "live out of control." I learned a great deal from this book and commend it strongly to the global Christian community.

—David P. Gushee, Distinguished University Professor
of Christian Ethics, Mercer University

In a time when much about our lives seems out of control, Rodney Clapp deftly explains that this, in fact, is our Christian calling, personally and collectively. Far from a posture of resignation or a relinquishing of agency, living out of control, he insists, is about embodying a lively and lifegiving witness that is shrewd in its assessment of systems of domination. Drawing on important work in prefigurative politics and Christian anarchism, Clapp paints a compelling picture of living out of control for the sake of the gospel and its good news for the oppressed and the suffering.

—Debra Dean Murphy, professor of religious studies and founder
of the Center for Restorative Justice, West Virginia Wesleyan
College; author of *Teaching That Transforms: Worship as the
Heart of Christian Formation*, and *Happiness, Health,
and Beauty: The Christian Life in Everyday Terms*

In this thoughtful and wide-ranging book, Rodney Clapp challenges Christians to take seriously the reality that Christendom is on the wane—that Christians *qua* Christians are not, will not be, and should not want to be in control of the American polity. His accessible, provocative reflections should spur conversation within congregations seeking to discern the shape of faithfulness to the gospel and among friends—inside and outside the church—in search of political integrity in the absence of control.

—Gary Chartier, associate dean and Distinguished Professor
of Law and Business Ethics, La Sierra University

Rodney Clapp has given us the book we all need at this moment. With vivid writing, theological depth, and an abundance of wisdom, *Living Out of Control* will help you make sense of this moment and hear again the call of Jesus Christ to follow within it. Timely and rich.

—Andrew Root, Carrie Olson Baalson Professor of Youth
and Family Ministry, Luther Seminary, and author
of *Evangelism in an Age of Despair*

Christians in the US are severely tempted to bind themselves to political parties and politicians in hopes of exerting and even recovering a measure of power and control. Seeking control, Christians ironically find themselves under the control of forces and movements ultimately opposed to the goals of the gospel. Rodney Clapp's *Living Out of Control* is a bracing call to Christians in the US to repent of their desires to control and to devote themselves to resisting the powers that seek to control them. This book is filled with probing insights, wise counsel, and careful judgments. These work together to call Christians to the place where they are most secure *because* they are most out of control: the act of worshipping in word and sacrament.

—Stephen Fowl, president and dean, Church
Divinity School of the Pacific

Beautifully and convincingly written, informative as well as inspiring. Live a free life, out of control, with another masterpiece by Rodney Clapp: *Living Out of Control*!

—Davor Džalto, professor at University College Stockholm,
president of the Institute for the Study of Culture and
Christianity, and author of *Anarchy and the Kingdom of God*

Rodney Clapp's account of a "waning" Christendom—changed, not ended—provides a sobering yet insightful, and ultimately encouraging, agenda for a changed church in a difficult world. Clapp envisages a different Christian practice, setting aside both the paternalism of past social witness and the attendant objectification of creation itself, in favor of recovering a "resonance" fitting to the needs of the world and to the changed reality of a Christian faith that has to rethink itself amid the secular. This significant, even profound achievement is the sketch of a Christian ethic that remains engaged and relevant to contemporary social and political practice, while avoiding the compromises of Christian nationalism as well as the self-indulgence of some "post-Christian" postures.

—Andrew McGowan, dean, Berkeley Divinity
School at Yale University

White Christians, long the controlling force in American society, became a minority of the population somewhere around 2015, and Christianity overall is steadily contracting in numbers and influence. Yet, to speak of a post-Christian nation—as some breathless commentators would have it—is inaccurate. In his characteristically thought-provoking way, Rodney Clapp depicts competing paths forward: on the one hand, a deeply problematic reassertion of the United States as a Christian nation, and on the other, a creative, fresh alternative unexpectedly drawing on Christian anarchists alongside gospel preaching, the Eucharist, and the virtue of friendship as sources for inhabiting this new reality of "being out of control." Highly recommended.

—Christian Scharen, associate professor and Gordon
Braatz Chair in Worship, Lutheran School
of Theology at Chicago

LIVING

OUT OF

CONTROL

Political & Personal Faith
in Waning Christendom

RODNEY CLAPP

FORTRESS PRESS
MINNEAPOLIS

LIVING OUT OF CONTROL
Political and Personal Faith in Waning Christendom

Copyright © 2025 by Fortress Press. All rights reserved. Except for brief
quotations in critical articles or reviews, no part of this book may be
reproduced in any manner without prior written permission from the
publisher. Email copyright@fortresspress.com or write to Permissions,
Fortress Press, PO Box 1209, Minneapolis, MN 55440-1209.

30   29   28   27   26   25   1   2   3   4   5   6   7   8   9

Library of Congress Cataloging-in-Publication Data

Names: Clapp, Rodney, author.
Title: Living out of control : political and personal faith in waning
   Christendom / Rodney Clapp.
Description: Minneapolis, MN : Fortress Press, [2025] | Includes
   bibliographical references.
Identifiers: LCCN 2024025694 (print) | LCCN 2024025695 (ebook) | ISBN
   9798889832249 (print) | ISBN 9798889832256 (ebook)
Subjects: LCSH: Christianity and politics--United States. | Christianity
   and culture--United States. | Christians--United States.
Classification: LCC BR526 .C568 2025 (print) | LCC BR526 (ebook) | DDC
   261.70973--dc23/eng/20240805
LC record available at https://lccn.loc.gov/2024025694
LC ebook record available at https://lccn.loc.gov/2024025695

Cover image: Empty boardwalk on a morning with dense fog, from
SanderStock/Getty Images
Cover design: Brice Hemmer

Print ISBN: 979-8-8898-3224-9
eBook ISBN: 979-8-8898-3225-6

For Mike Budde, friend who has taught me much
about politics and faithful living

Contents

Acknowledgments

As the footnotes attest, I have learned much from many scholars and church leaders. Behind the book, however, and not so in evidence, are debts owed to astute friends who took the time to critically read my manuscript in early drafts. I am grateful to John Armstrong, Mike Budde, Stan Hauerwas, and B. J. Heyboer, who fulfilled that crucial role in the making of this book. On occasion they corrected me; always they helped sharpen what I wanted to say.

This is my second book with the esteemed Fortress Press. Again, I have benefited from the faithful sponsorship and careful editing of Ryan Hemmer. Lisa Eaton oversaw the copyediting and Carrie Bond read finely, minutely, and excellently. I am grateful to all of the Fortress staff for helping produce such a beautiful physical object. Long live the old-fashioned book! And it will so long as publishers as skilled and dedicated as Fortress exist.

In some countries they do not ask, "Where do you go to church?" but "Where do you pray?" My primary place of prayer for the last forty-years-plus has been St. Barnabas Episcopal Church, in Glen Ellyn, Illinois. My wife and I have practically grown up there. No church is flawless, but St. Barnabas has been steadily faithful and consistently good to us. The people who make and are this church are close to our hearts and have taught us much. We are thankful to them, and not least to the succession of priests who have shepherded St. Barnabas while we have been there: Father Robert Macfarlane, Father Matthew Gunter (now bishop of Wisconsin), Mother Natalie Beam Van Kirk, and most recently Father Timothy O'Leary, who never tires in reminding Christians how indelibly Jewish we are. Recent circumstances are moving us from St. Barnabas to some yet undetermined church in Oregon. We can only hope and pray for a place and people half so nourishing to us as St. Barnabas.

My primary daily nourishers are my wife, Sandy, and our dog, Ury. With her faithfulness, generativity, humor, and patience, Sandy keeps me well and helps me rise to whatever level of excellence I may manage. Ury, a chocolate miniature labradoodle, greets every new day with gusto and amuses us constantly with his liveliness, orneriness, and curiosity. No writing, let alone living, could ever get done, at least not so joyfully, without these two remarkable mainstays who have made me their best friend.

CHAPTER ONE

After Christendom or Waning Christendom?

People do not like to live out of control. We feel most at ease when we control not just ourselves but others who exist alongside us. Slavery and other persistent oppressions—patriarchy, structural racism, wars of conquest—demonstrate as much. For a long time in Europe and America, Christians have been in control. We have lived comfortably in the state called Christendom—that time and place in which Christianity prevails. It is a time and place in which everyone is assumed to be a Christian unless demonstrated otherwise. It is a time and place where government and culture are guided and suffused, at least nominally, by Christian faith.

Christendom runs deep. Our calendars hinge, from BCE to CE, around the date of Jesus's lifetime. The Sabbath, except in Jewish and Muslim enclaves, falls on Sunday, the Christian day of worship—and the weekends that free most of us from work and for leisure were built around Sabbath concepts.

Christendom perhaps reached its high point in the United States in the 1950s. It was in 1954 that the Pledge of Allegiance, with its rewritten "one nation *under God*," was instituted in schools and public assemblies. In the 1950s churches were proliferating and full. Businesses closed on Sundays and "blue laws" prohibited the Sunday sales of alcohol. Embroiled in a cold war with so-called "godless" communists, the nation consciously and fervently considered itself oppositional as "Christian."

But now Christendom is fading and besieged. I do not think I need to belabor this point. Both Christians and non-Christians of various types agree on it. Christianity, in any substantive sense, is not delineated as our governmental authority. High and popular culture do not assume the reality and influence of the Christian God.

Maybe we can clarify the point by borrowing from historian Gary Gerstle's concept of a "political order." For Gerstle, a political order is a longstanding "constellation of ideologies, policies, and constituencies" that prevails over any and all other competitors.[1] The New Deal era, arising in the 1930s, cresting in the 1950s and 1960s, and falling in the 1970s, is a premier example of a political order. For nearly a half-century, the concepts, leaders, and policies of the New Deal set the terms of debate. As Gerstle writes, "The prestige of the New Deal was such that the Republican Party, when it finally regained the White House in 1952, acquiesced to its core principles. As Dwight D. Eisenhower's presidency unfolded, it became apparent that the New Dealers had bent him and other Republicans to their will, structuring the very terrain on which the latter were compelled to fight. The ability of a partisan political movement to define the parameters of American politics in enduring ways indicates the presence of a political order."[2]

I suggest we may think of Christendom as an order—not just a political but also a cultural order. As such an order, Christendom is done. Christianity no longer sets the terms of political, social, and cultural debate. It no longer structures the very terrain on which all others are compelled to fight. Consequently, many theologians and other thinkers have talked about us living "after Christendom." I am one of them, having written a book subtitled *Christian Culture in a Post-Christian Society.*[3]

---

1 Gary Gerstle, *The Rise and Fall of the Neoliberal Order: America and the World in the Free Market Era* (New York: Oxford University Press, 2022), 2.

2 Gerstle, *Rise and Fall,* 20.

3 See Rodney Clapp, *A Peculiar People: The Church as Culture in a Post-Christian Society* (Downers Grove, IL: InterVarsity, 1996).

But now I believe those of us who have declared the end of Christendom were a little over hasty and were overly generalizing. I have not changed my mind on the end of Christendom as a political and cultural order. Christianity no longer rules, can no longer simply be assumed. Yet that does not mean all marks of Christendom have been obliterated. Nor have all proponents of Christendom died off. The New Deal again provides a helpful analogy. As an order, the New Deal is done. But Franklin Delano Roosevelt, the main architect of the New Deal, remains widely venerated. And there are still those vying to revive the New Deal's principles and reinstate it: for instance, they work for stronger welfare policies and higher tax rates on the wealthy.[4]

Likewise, Christendom, however beleaguered, has its backers—including estimable theologians.[5] They may be dismissed in some quarters as atavistic, but they are steadily and spiritedly striving to restore or reinvigorate Christendom. Many want America to be declared and reembodied as a Christian nation. As I said, being out of control can be uncomfortable—and being in control is a longtime habit for American Christians. It is not a habit easily broken. Or, to change the metaphor, it is, like the kudzu so preponderant in the South, not a plant easy to eliminate. You can spray it, uproot it, try to tear it out of the powerlines and trees, but it will keep coming back.

CHRISTIANITY BY THE NUMBERS

Fifty years ago, the number of Americans calling themselves Christian was 90 percent.[6] Now that figure is at 64 percent. And a 2021

---

4 See, for example, Thom Hartmann, *The Hidden History of Neoliberalism: How Reaganism Gutted America and How to Restore Its Greatness* (New York: Berrett-Koehler, 2022).

5 See Oliver O'Donovan's *The Desire of the Nations: Rediscovering the Roots of Political Theology* (Cambridge: Cambridge University Press, 1996).

6 The figures in this section, unless noted otherwise, may be found in Pew Research Center, "Modeling the Future of Religion," https:www.pewresearch.org/religion/2022/09/13/modeling-the-future-of-religion-in-America/.

Gallup Poll revealed that church membership, which may be one indicator of how seriously people live their faith, had fallen below 50 percent.[7] Meanwhile, as has been ubiquitously reported, "nones," or the religiously unaffiliated, have risen sharply in recent years, now accounting for 30 percent of the US population.

Furthermore, the future trends toward a continued decline of professing (let alone active) Christians and an increase of "nones." The Pew Research Center imagines four possible scenarios for the next five decades. Noting that an increasing number of young people (those under age thirty) are now "switching" out of Christianity, the first scenario postulates that if switching continues at its current pace, Christians would dip below 50 percent of the population by 2060, and by 2070 would compose 46 percent of the population. The second scenario posits that switching would speed up initially but then hold steady. Under this scenario, Christians would lose their majority status by 2050. And by 2070 "nones" would constitute a plurality of 48 percent, with Christians accounting for 39 percent of all Americans. The third scenario imagines that switching would ramp up throughout the next five decades. Then Christians, at 43 percent, would no longer be a majority by 2045. And "nones," at 52 percent, would compose a majority of citizens. Finally, the fourth scenario pictures the switching phenomenon screeching to a halt, immediately. Only then would Christians retain their majority status, at 54 percent, by the year 2070.

In sum, Christianity might lose its majority status by as early as 2045, in just twenty years. And it is all but certain to lose that status by 2070. I say "all but certain" because history is not simply predictable. Massive religious revival, for example, cannot be ruled out. Thomas Jefferson predicted in the 1820s that Christianity in the United States would be replaced by an "enlightened" form of religion

---

7 John Blake, "Predictions about the Decline of Christianity in America May be Premature," CNN (April 9, 2023), https://www.cnn.com/2023/04/08/us/christianity-decline-easter-blake-cec/index.html.

that jettisoned belief in Jesus's divinity and miracles. The subsequent Second Great Awakening, among other things, proved him wrong.[8] But barring something like the kind of miracle Jefferson was eager to reject—a massive revival—we can only expect more decline of Christianity in America.

Still, even assuming the death of Christendom as a political and social order, revenants of Christendom will not soon disappear. Consider that while losing its majority, Christianity will remain a significant plurality. Even 46 percent of the population would represent a formidable, even overwhelming, voting bloc. Of course, Christians do not vote as a monolithic bloc. Yet the near unanimity of evangelicalism as a voting bloc, for example, formed a winning base for Donald Trump in 2016. And the cultural power of Christianity remains strong and vital. To take another evangelical example, we need only consider how dispensationalism's rapture theology has suffused the popular imagination, taking form not only in churches but in the Marvel Comic Universe and in "peak" television shows such as *The Leftovers*.[9]

So I suggest it is most precise and helpful to speak not of "post-Christendom" or as if we are totally "after Christendom." We might rather see Christendom as waning. If it is waning, it is weakened, but we still live with and within its effects. Christendom is not and will not die with a whimper. The question is what Christians will do, how we will live and witness, within waning Christendom.

---

8 Blake, "Predictions about the Decline of Christianity."

9 For an astute discussion of the subtleties and challenges of even a waning Christendom, see Jason Mahn, *Becoming a Christian in Christendom: Radical Discipleship and the Way of the Cross in America's "Christian" Culture* (Minneapolis: Fortress, 2016). For example, as Mahn notes Ron Adams's and Isaac Villegas's warning, "To proclaim Christendom's death prematurely only serves to mask all the ways we benefit from the institutional prominence of cultural Christianity as it shapes our society." This is, as Mahn remarks, "a form of Christianity that has accommodated to every other aspect of culture, thus making it all too easy to 'pass' as a Christian" (14).

THREE INHERENT TENSIONS WITHIN
AMERICAN CHRISTENDOM

As American Christendom wanes, it may look as if it is only being battered and attacked from outside it. This is the popular image that proponents of Christendom promote. The surrounding culture, they say, is decadent and turning or falling away from Christianity. Those most agitated against it—whether they come under "secular humanists" or another label—are actively chipping away at the Christian heritage and devastating the nation in the process. But in fact, there are deep tensions and fissures *within* American Christendom, inherent to it. To see and understand those tensions, we must know a bit about the republican theology American Christendom embodies.

Republican theology is not identical to or coterminous with the modern Republican Party, though it is now most comfortably situated there. Instead, republican (with a small "r") theology is an ideology that stems from the belief that America is a, if not *the,* "chosen nation." It also focuses on republican liberty and limited government. Such republican liberty is liberty guarded and promulgated by freely chosen representatives of a free people. This republican theology, fusing free-market values with traditional morality, is what the political scientist Benjamin Lynerd calls "quasi-libertarian."[10] It is libertarian to the extent that it favors small or limited government, serving a closely circumscribed role and leaving individuals unburdened to pursue the aims and dreams of their separate lives. But it is *quasi*-libertarian in that it urges what it takes as traditional morality, and in fact wants government to legislate and otherwise support that morality. Such moralizing intent makes republican theology prone to expect government to move far beyond the narrow roles of national defense, policing, and the protection of private property. Unlike strict libertarians, republican theologians and their quasi-libertarian followers want government to step up on such "private"

---

10 Benjamin T. Lynerd, *Republican Theology: The Civil Religion of American Evangelicals* (Oxford: Oxford University Press, 2014), 3.

matters as alcohol consumption, drug use, pornography, abortion, and same-sex relationships.

We cannot properly understand republican theology without appreciating the role revivals have played in its history and formulation. Revivals aim to win individual "souls," preaching and repeating hymns or praise songs as one person after another walks to the altar or raises a hand of assent. This one-person-at-a-time approach then supposedly leads to not only private but social transformation. Win enough individual souls, and pretty soon a city, a state, a nation will be changed. Likewise, republican theology has focused on individuals and individual change.

The revivalist anthropology, or understanding of the human, has resulted in an inherent tension within American Christendom. So focused on the individual, this theology has largely been blind to structural injustice.[11] Republican theology and its followers were reluctant latecomers, then, to the civil rights movement and its associated structural transformations. And a blindness, or at least myopia, about structural realities still makes it hard for those who view reality through the lens of republican theology to see how a capitalist political economy shapes people first and foremost as self-centered consumers, eroding self-restraint and the ability to care for others as well as any vestige of a common good.

As I have already hinted, the quasi-libertarianism of republican theology is a second tension immanent to American Christendom. On some fronts, republican theologians and their backers sound like full-throated libertarians. But, in fact, they combine a "libertarian ethos" with "restrictive public moralism."[12] Republican theology is at odds with itself on this point. Accordingly, it should come as little surprise that critics often call out evangelicals, our most prominent modern adherents of republican theology, for advocating small government except when it comes to people's "personal" or "private" lives.

---

11 See Lynerd, *Republican Theology*, 9.

12 Lynerd, *Republican Theology*, 4.

Finally, the third and most significant inherent tension in American Christendom returns us to the roots of republican theology: the confusion of the church and its mission with the American nationalist project. Positing America as *a* or *the* chosen nation misconstrues the biblical role of Israel as the uniquely chosen nation and fails to appreciate that the New Testament writings were addressed not to any nation but to ecclesial bodies. It also misappropriates early American history, most notably the Puritan John Winthrop and his famous reference to a "city on a hill."

Winthrop's words emerged from his sermon *A Model of Christian Charity.* The shining, testimonial "city on hill" he had in mind was not America as a nascent nation but the church. It is forgotten that Winthrop settled his Massachusetts Bay colony with a congregation of one thousand followers. And, as the historian Abram Van Engen puts it, for Winthrop and company the "chosen" were those who were "called out (ecclesia), [who] were always understood to be the whole church—all the saints, all the godly, all the gatherings of the faithful in all the parts of the world wherever the Lord had appointed them to dwell, whether in England, New England, the Netherlands, or elsewhere. Winthrop and his followers never believed that God had set them apart single-handedly to save the world." Winthrop's "was an international conception—a communion of saints never limited to the American strand."[13]

Even as recently as the early decades of the twentieth century, Winthrop's "city on a hill" was understood to primarily describe "disciples, apostles, churches, preachers, Christians, missionaries, and so forth. . . . In other words, for most of American history, when people heard the words 'city on a hill,' [originally drawn, of course, from Matthew 5:14], they were discussing discipleship, not citizenship. It took the cultural work of scholars and politicians, dedicated to diverse projects over many years, to turn a phrase of the church

---

13 Abram C. Van Engen, *City on a Hill: A History of American Exceptionalism* (New Haven, CT: Yale University Press, 2020), 45, 267.

into the definition of a nation."[14] The appropriation of the churchly "city on a hill" to designate the American national project reached its apogee in 1974, when Ronald Reagan used the phrase to argue that "by a Divine plan this nation was placed between two oceans to be sought out by those with a special brand of courage and love of freedom."[15]

Whatever its innate tensions, many today are struggling to re-enliven Christendom: their answer to living out of control is reasserting Christendom, getting back in control. The book in your hands represents a different response. In it, I remember that much, even most, of the Bible depicts faith communities (first Jewish, then Christian) living out of control of their culture and politics. But these communities did not live without agency, without a real ability to act in and influence their worlds. And they did not live without hope in the living God. Here, I will try to capture the imagination, to present a different and better story than, say, Christian nationalists, about the possibilities of living out of control. We will reconsider responsibility as response-ability, introduce prefigurative politics, cheer on a kind of Christian anarchism, remind ourselves of resonance with others and with the world that can only be realized by accepting that we are not in control, hold up the massive potential of friendship in a lonely and desperate society, and lift up again the ongoing riches of celebrating the Eucharist and proclaiming the gospel.

---

14 Van Engen, *City on a Hill*, 8.
15 Cited in Van Engen, *City on a Hill*, 272.

CHAPTER TWO

Responsibility as Response-ability

I declare *responsibility* a dirty word. Especially when it denotes paternalistic responsibility *for* other adults, rather than a codetermining responsibility *to* or *with* them, responsibility is a dangerous and objectionable concept. Such responsibility is all about being in control. A fitting name for it is imperialism; yet another, colonialism; and yet one more, racism.

In 1899, the British author Rudyard Kipling starkly manifested all three aspects of this reality with his poem "The White Man's Burden: The United States and The Philippine Islands." Kipling wrote in light of the Philippine-American War and the eventual treaty that subjugated Puerto Rico, Guam, Cuba, and the Philippines to American control. Famously, he looked on these and other imperial subjects as "fluttered [spineless?] folk and wild— / Your new-caught, sullen peoples, / Half devil and half child." He exhorted Americans, following the conduct of the British and other Europeans, to "Take up the White Man's burden," purportedly bettering, civilizing, and liberating from darkness the fickle and feckless citizens of other races and nations. Since the subjects balked and resisted, to be sure, this was a heavy duty, a dire responsibility demanding that Americans "search your manhood" and bear up "Through all the thankless years." But only so would they merit a kindly "judgment of your peers!"[1]

---

1 Rudyard Kipling, "The White Man's Burden: The United States and The Philippine Islands," https://historymatters.gmu.edu/d/5478/.

Yet, as I hinted in my first paragraph, there is another way to construe responsibility. Rather than paternalistic (and easily self-deceived) responsibility *for*, it may be understood as responsibility *to* and *with* others.[2] This latter is responsibility as response-ability. It is the capacity and skill to look intently, listen closely, and accordingly, genuinely respond to the other—just as they in turn, in any healthy relationship, will respond to you. It is a way to live nonmanipulatively, respectfully, and effectively out of control.

In this sense *responsibility* is not an ethical exhortation, like Kipling's charge to live up to the judgment of peers, or like an exasperated parent's cry to "Be responsible and pick up your room!" It is much more basic than that. Responsibility as response-ability is an anthropological fact, that, at rock bottom it is what makes us human, what constitutes us as selves. We are born into responsive relationships and we develop as persons through reacting to those relationships, first to a mother, then to a father, and eventually to communities of learning and socialization, as well as the languages and lifeways of the cultures in which we are immersed. Responsibility as response-ability makes us what and who we are. So this responsibility is not—first and foremost—an ethical demand we choose or refuse. Quite simply, to be a self is to be, initially and ongoingly, responsible, that is, response-able.[3]

RESPONSIBILITY AND CREATION

In the Jewish and Christian stories, humans (and indeed the rest of creation) are created and intended to live responsibly in just this sense. The first creation story (Gen 1:1–2:4a) depicts a God who shares power, invites creatures to engage in a real degree of cocreation, and

---

2 I say "easily self-deceived" because what imperialists often wanted, more than any supposed "bettering" of their subjects, was the gold or other resources beneath their land, or strategic locales for military bases.

3 James W. Fowler, *To See the Kingdom: The Theological Vision of H. Richard Niebuhr* (Lanham, MD: University Press of America, 1974), 154.

seeds creation with open-ended potential. Genesis 1 proceeds with a series of permissions and enablement for creation's response-able development. The Hebrew grammar, happily not lost in English translation, emphasizes creation's responsible involvement, its robust participation, in the process of creation.

Notice the series of *Lets*. "Let the earth put forth vegetation . . ." (v. 11). "Let the waters bring forth swarms of living creatures . . ." (v. 20). "Let the earth bring forth living creatures of every kind . . ." (v. 24). Earth and waters are first given the potential to produce, to populate, to luxuriate, and then given permission to "put forth" and "bring forth" vegetation, swarms of living creatures of every kind. Earth and waters have God-given drives and capacities for the cascading unfolding, the ongoing blooming, of creation. And God calls for them—allows for them—to unleash those drives and capacities.

God assigns humankind a key role in the creative process. Creating humanity expressly in God's image, and as male and female, God pronounces, "Let them have dominion over the fish of the sea, and over the birds of the air, and over the cattle, and over all the wild animals of the earth, and over every creeping thing that creeps upon the earth" (Gen 1:26). This text has been exploited on behalf of earth's exploitation. Humanity's "dominion" has been read as permission, or even a mandate, for humans to do whatever they like with other creatures, and indeed to lord it over them, harvest, slaughter, and abuse them at will.

But there is another, and arguably more fitting, way to read the text. Notice that in context we have already seen God sharing the power of creation with God's creatures. Earth and waters are given potential and then permission to bring forth all sorts of life. Now God shares some of this same power with humans, granting them power and place to direct the ongoing, unfolding future of all swimming, flying, prancing, and creeping creatures. This is a God who allots power to creatures, a God who does not simply exercise overwhelming force but invites creatures to exercise power alongside and with God. This is the God in whose image humans are created. "Dominion," accordingly, should be tempered and redirected to nurture and not annihilation, to caretaking and not exploitation.

The biblical scholar Terence Fretheim puts it well. "If the God portrayed in Genesis 1 is understood only or fundamentally in terms of overwhelming power, absolute control, and independent, unilateral activity, then those who are created in God's image could *properly* understand their creaturely role in comparable terms. In such an understanding, the relationship of God's image to the rest of creation is to be one of power over, absolute control, and independence. By definition, the natural world becomes available for human manipulation and exploitation."[4] But clearly, the God of Genesis 1 is not concerned with overwhelming power, absolute control, and independent, unilateral activity. Instead, the God pictured there chooses collaborative power in relationship, to create creatures capable of response-ability, and to let their responses play an integral hand in the life and direction of ongoing creation. In short, "God is a power-sharing God, and God will be faithful to that way of relating to those created in the divine image."[5]

The second creation story (Gen 2:4b–25) similarly depicts God sharing the power and potential of creation with that very creation. God here consults with the first human about what may be a fitting partner and companion for him (2:18–23). God parades animals of the field and birds from the air, but the human considers none fully or profoundly suitable. Then the first woman is created, and man has at last found a fitting companion. So God, as Fretheim says, has let the human being determine "whether the animals or the woman is adequate" to be a profound companion. "The human being, not God, deems what is 'fit for him.' The future of the human race in some basic respect lies in human hands. . . . God so values human freedom that God will take into account the free human response from within the creative process in shaping the future."[6]

The naming of the animals episode (Gen 2:19–20) stands significantly in the same regard. As Fretheim comments, "Naming is part

4 Terence E. Fretheim, *God and World in the Old Testament: A Relational Theology of Creation* (Nashville: Abingdon, 2005), 49.

5 Fretheim, *God and World*, 49.

6 Fretheim, *God and World*, 57.

of the creative process itself, discerning the very nature of intracrea-turely relationships. Human decisions are shown to be important in the ongoing development of the created order. It is not that human beings have the capacity to stymie God's movement into the future in any *final* way, but God has established a relationship with human beings such that their decisions about the creation truly count."[7]

In short, the God with whom we have to do is not a control freak. Instead, this God shapes and molds a creation that plays a signifi-cant hand in its own future. This God creates a response-able cre-ation, expecting creatures to respond to God's initiative. And this is especially true of people, all created in God's image, and, like God, expected to leave room for other creatures to develop and participate in their destiny. Thus, humans are not fundamentally independent, atomized individuals, in unending and basic competition with one another and brutal rule over the rest of creation. Instead, they—we—are *interdependent* and *interconnected*, called to responsibility to and with God, one another, and the rest of creation.[8] As such we can live—and flourish—out of control.

In such an attitude, orientation, or disposition, we see in others the very possibility of being a self and a person. And in a community constituted by and constituting such selves, we meet limits, but gra-cious limits, on our individual wills. Otherwise, we are inclined to desire domination and treating the other manipulatively, as only a means or vehicle to our own ends and selfish aims.

This and much more is reflected in the Hebrew word for "respon-sibility," *acharayut*, whose root *acher* means "other." The Jewish philosopher David Patterson expounds:

---

7 Fretheim, *God and World*, 58. Regarding the naming of the animals, ecotheologian Norman Wirzba comments that Adam's naming was not so that he might dominate the creatures, but so that he might discern "how best to relate to each animal." Noman Wirzba, *This Sacred Life: Humanity's Place in a Wounded World* (Cambridge: Cambridge University Press, 2021), 20.

8 The Baptist theologian Myles Werntz ably argues that in distinction from isolated individuals, we are persons, "the interconnected creatures of God." Myles Werntz, *From Isolation to Community: A Renewed Vision for Christian Life Together* (Grand Rapids: Baker Academic, 2022), 41.

This Hebrew word confirms what I have tried to convey, namely that the responsibility that lays claim to me comes not from within myself, not from what I think or feel, but it descends upon me from on high, as revealed in the face of the other human being. Because only *I* can meet *this* responsibility, my responsibility is what defines who I am. Which means: I am the "not-I"—the "other," the *acher* in my *acharayut*. That is why when I fail in my *acharayut*, I become *acher* to myself, "other" than who I am, hence absent from my fellow human being. Absent from my fellow human being, I have no time, a point underscored by the verb *achar,* meaning to "be late," to "tarry," or to "lag behind," and by the noun *acharit*, which means "end" or "future." The other human being *is* my end, *is* my future—*is* my meaning. Hence only through the responsibility that defines me do I generate a presence before the other, where I have time because I am on time—for the *relationship* that decides who I am.[9]

I quote Patterson at some length because his musings indicate how deeply grounded in the very Hebrew, biblical grammar is the understanding that selves necessarily exist in relation to other selves, and his musings also suggest responsibility exactly as response-ability. This responsibility is not something the individual creates or finds simply within himself or herself. Rather, it descends "from on high," in relationship with God, and is "revealed in the face of the other human being," in honest encounter with the neighbor or, Jesus will suggest, the enemy. When we fail to live responsibly, we are manifestly absent from neighbor or enemy. We are tardy at arriving for our own end or future, which is found only in coordination or even confrontation with the other. Alternatively, arriving on time to our encounter with another—meeting our responsibility—allows

---

9 David Patterson, *Eighteen Words to Sustain a Life: A Jewish Father's Ethical Will* (Eugene, OR: Cascade, 2023), 89–90.

us to "generate a presence." And this is a being present to the very *"relationship* that decides who I am."

Unfortunately, modernity has coached us to attempt to achieve an autonomous self, that is, a self in no need of interconnection with others. Modernity has largely defined reason and rationality as instrumental and autonomous, reason deployed as a means to master and possess other persons and the rest of creation.[10] Patterson unearths deep biblical roots, roots inherent to the very vocabulary and grammar, that instead picture reason as other-grounded and other-directed, intended to help us meet our glorious human potential not in defeating or exceeding others, but in flourishing with them. The missiologist and theologian Lesslie Newbigin neatly captures the contrasts between these two different renditions of reason. What we are here referring to as Hebrew reason "has become the servant of a listening and trusting openness instead of being the servant of a [modern] masterful autonomy. The difference is not between the use of reason and its abandonment; it is the difference between two ways of understanding the world, one in which the self is sovereign and the other in which I understand myself only in a relation of mutuality with other selves."[11]

THE LOGIC OF LIVING OUT OF CONTROL

God is pervasively present to all creation but does choose at times to be more intensively and dramatically present. God's power is

---

10 Historian Brad Gregory observes that the Enlightenment, over the last two to three centuries, operated "with the human resolve to take history under human administration and control—deploying for that purpose reason, believed to be the most powerful among human weapons (indeed, a flawless human facility to know, to predict, to calculate, and so to raise the 'is' to the level of the 'ought')." Brad S. Gregory, *The Unintended Reformation: How a Religious Revolution Secularized Society* (Cambridge, MA: The Belknap Press of Harvard University Press, 2012), 382.

11 Lesslie Newbigin, *The Gospel in a Pluralist Society* (Grand Rapids: Eerdmans, 1989), 61.

almighty, to be sure, and at times God chooses to break into creation with displays of this almighty power, with spectacularly constructive or even destructive results. We can think of episodes such as the vanquishing of the Egyptian army at the Red Sea. Or, as Christians, we think especially of the incarnation and the mystery of God become human in Jesus of Nazareth.

Yet, centrally and decisively, what God desires is a real relationship—a free, trusting, responsive relationship—with human beings. We are not created to be cowering vassals or abject slaves or mere puppets. So God restrains and puts in reserve God's almighty, overwhelming power. God makes room for the Israelites to choose for or against God's call to covenant relationship. "I call heaven and earth to witness against you today that I have before you life and death, blessings and curses. Choose life so that you and your descendants may live . . ." (Deut 30:19; see also, e.g., Josh 24:15). In terms of the incarnation, God become human does not wipe out all enemies but dies vulnerably on a cross. Nor does Jesus comprehensively and sweepingly heal all sickness; instead he chooses to heal particular people who respond in trust and faith. Jesus performs signs and wonders and leaves others to interpret and respond—or not—to those signs and wonders. Significantly, when Satan tempts Jesus with implacable and unchallengeable political power over all the earth, Jesus roundly rejects the temptation (Matt 4:8–10).

To introduce a parallel from sacramental theology, just as Christ is present in, with, and under the elements and actions of the Eucharist, so God works in, with, and under human actions and the unfolding of history. God operates "without micromanagement, tight control, or interference every time something goes wrong."[12] Again, this is because God desires responsive and responsible relationship with human beings. Ultimately, we must speak of faith (trust) and especially love. "For God to have forced compliance to the divine will and not allowed creatures the freedom to fail would have been to deny

---

12 Fretheim, *God and World*, 7.

any genuine relationship."[13] Just as we cannot create love by coercion in a romantic relationship, love cannot be coerced into existence in our relationship to the divine.

To be crystal clear, I am not denying that the biblical God is almighty. But we need to get straight how God exercises almighty power. As the liturgical occasion declares, "O God, you declare your almighty power chiefly in showing mercy and pity . . ."[14] The French sociologist and theologian Jacques Ellul puts it just right: "Though the biblical God is almighty, in practice he does not make use of his omnipotence in his dealings with us except in particular instances which are recorded precisely because they are abnormal (e.g., the Flood, the Tower of Babel, or Sodom and Gomorrah). God's is a self-limited omnipotence, not through caprice or fancy, but because anything else would be in contradiction to his very being [and relational aims with humanity]. For beyond power, the dominant and conditioning fact is that the being of God is love." Further, says Ellul, "If we accept that God is love, and that it is human beings who are to respond to this love, the explanation for [God's normal self-limitation and human freedom] is simple. Love cannot be forced, ordered, or made obligatory. It is necessarily free. If God liberates, it is because he expects and hopes that we will come to know him and love him. He cannot lead us to do so by terrorizing us."[15] A God of naked, unrestrained, unqualified, and overwhelming power—in short—is not the God of Israel and Jesus Christ.

Accordingly, the Bible pictures a God who works by what we might call a narrative logic. Stories always concern particular people and events, and pivot on particular choices. Likewise, God works redemption by choosing (electing) a particular man, Abraham, and calling him into a responsive relationship. Working in, with, and under Abraham, God will create a nation more numerous than the

---

13 Fretheim, *God and World,* 70.

14 Book of Common Prayer (The Epsicopal Church; New York: Oxford University Press, 1990), Proper 21, 234.

15 Jacques Ellul, *Anarchy and Christianity* (Grand Rapids: Eerdmans, 1991), 33, 39.

sands of the seashore, through which all the earth will be redeemed (Gen 22:17; 26:4). Then God will work through the Jewish people to make his ways known. And at last, God will choose a particular Jew, Jesus, through which to save and liberate all creation. The German theologian Gerhard Lohfink nicely expresses the flow and purpose of this biblical narrative logic.

> How can anyone change the world and society at its roots without taking away freedom? It can only be that God begins in a small way, at one single place in the world. There must be a place, visible, tangible, where the salvation of the world can begin: that is, where the world becomes what it is supposed to be according to God's plan. Beginning at that place, the new thing can spread abroad, but only through persuasion, not through indoctrination, not through violence. Everyone must have an opportunity to come and see. All must have the chance to behold and test this new thing. Then, if they want to, they can allow themselves to be drawn into the history of salvation that God is creating. . . . What drives them to the new thing cannot be force, not even moral pressure, but only the fascination of a world that is changed.[16]

So the God met in Israel and Jesus Christ reveals God's nature and character, and they are seen to be grounded in God's desire for responsible relationship with God's creation. That entails freedom from coercion. And just as God relinquishes a degree (or a kind) of control, the church is meant to live out of control. The church's only recourse and intention, in fulfilling its mission in the world, is persuasion. The church hence seeks to be, in and through God's grace, a source of fascination amid the world. At its best, the church arouses curiosity and ignites questions. Rather than being a controlling, coercive force in the world, through the Holy Spirit it embodies the

---

16 Gerhard Lohfink, *Does God Need the Church? Toward a Theology of the People of God* (Collegeville, MN: Michael Glazer, 1999), 27.

beauty of community—of people living for God and one another—in a riven, polarized world. Fascination and beauty can be endlessly and astonishingly compelling, but they are never compulsory. God calls us to live responsibly and out of control in just this fashion.

The revealed character of God, and the patience, persuasion, and nonviolence it entailed for the church's mission, was apparent to the early, pre- and even incipient Constantinian church. Thus writes Irenaeus (second to third century): God works "by means of persuasion . . . [God] does not use violent means to obtain what he desires." Similarly, the author of *The Epistle to Diognetus* (second to third century) avers that God in sending Christ "willed to save man by persuasion, not by compulsion, for compulsion is not God's way of working." And Lactantius (third to fourth century) comments: "Religion must be defended not by killing but by dying, not by violence but by patience."[17]

A NIEBUHRIAN ASSIST

An exemplary way to encapsulate responsibility as response-ability, and its entailment for the church's role in the world, is to revisit the work of the twentieth-century American theologian H. Richard Niebuhr. In 1963's *The Responsible Self,* Niebuhr argues for the socially constituted self. Then, driving to the heart of the Christian ethic, Niebuhr places responsibility at the center. He writes: "What is implicit in the idea of responsibility is the image of man-the-answerer, man reacting in response to action upon him."[18] The human is the response-able creature, and the first one to whom the human has to respond is his or her Creator, Sustainer, Judge, and Redeemer. In creating, in sustaining, in judging, in redeeming,

---

17 All cited in Alan Kreider, *The Patient Ferment of the Early Church: The Improbable Rise of Christianity in the Roman Empire* (Grand Rapids: Baker Academic, 2016), 120. Kreider's entire book is outstandingly helpful on this subject.

18 H. Richard Niebuhr, *The Responsible Self: An Essay in Christian Moral Philosophy* (New York: Harper and Row, 1963), 56.

God is always the initiating agent. We humans respond to these
initiating and preceding acts and communications of God. But no
one of us does so alone. As the Niebuhr commentator James Fowler
says, our "relations to objects, other persons, to ideas, are always
qualified by [our] relations to companions—co-knowers, co-valuers,
co-interpreters in communities of interpretation."[19] The church is
one such community of interpretation—for Christians, the *premier*
community of interpretation. It is in and through the church, after
all, that we learn to pray, to read the Scripture, to serve one another
and the world, to heed tradition and history, and to employ the
Christian vocabulary and grammar.

Since we are fundamentally responding and responsible selves,
our first question in determining the direction of our lives and any
particular action is not "What should we do?" Rather, says Niebuhr,
the prior question is "What is going on?" Put theistically, the question,
referring to the initiating, preceding, creating and redeeming Agent
working in, under, and with the universe, is "What is God doing?"
Niebuhr thinks this pattern of responsibility is borne out by a reading of Scripture as a whole. "At the critical junctures in the history
of Israel and the early Christian community the decisive question
men raised was not 'What is the goal?' nor yet 'What is the law?' but
'What is happening?' and then 'What is the fitting response to what
is happening?'" Accordingly, "Israel is the people that is to see and
understand the action of God in everything that happens and to
make a fitting reply. So it is in the New Testament also. The God to
whom Jesus points is not the commander who gives laws but the doer
of small and of mighty deeds, the creator of sparrows and clother of
lilies, the ultimate giver of blindness and sight, the ruler whose rule is
hidden in the manifold activities of plural agencies but is yet in a way
visible to those who know how to interpret the signs of the times."[20]

More specifically, Niebuhr would point to the story of Joseph:
thrown in a pit by his brothers, then enslaved in Egypt, with God

19 Fowler, *To See the Kingdom*, 154.
20 Niebuhr, *Responsible Self*, 63, 67.

working through these dire circumstances to bring Joseph to a position of later rescuing a famine-struck, starving Israel. He would point to Isaiah 10, where Assyria intends Israel's destruction, but God uses Assyria to draw Israel from its own self-destruction. And supremely, he would point to the crucifixion of Jesus, where priests, nationalists, Judas, Caiaphas, and Pilate thought simply to do evil, but God worked in, under, and through the total context to bring about the supreme good, the redemption of the world.[21] For Niebuhr Jesus is the preeminently responsible person, always loyal to the God of Israel, always first and foremost asking, in any challenge he faces or any suffering that befalls him, "What is happening? What is God doing?" Thus Jesus "interprets all actions upon him as signs of the divine action of creation, government, and salvation and so responds to them as to respond to divine action. He does that act which fits into the divine action and looks forward to the infinite response to his response."[22]

To ask, "What is God doing?" surely impinges most acutely in situations of suffering. When cancer invades, when a tornado or tsunami strikes, when poverty prevails, when a war breaks out, "What is God doing?" can become a prayer or even a tormented protest. For then we are in pain and under the sway of hurtful forces out of our control. Niebuhr avers that the character of people has been determined in no small part by their suffering, and more especially by their *responses* to suffering. "[I]t is in the response to suffering that many and perhaps all men, individually and in their groups, define themselves, take on character, develop their ethos."[23] If Niebuhr is right, and if suffering is in part a matter of being out of control, we need to ask "What is God doing?" in, with, and under waning Christendom. Are we, for example, being called back to a faith and way and life that is patient, peaceable, and non-coercive? Does the waning of Christendom hurt because it really is disastrous for God's work with the world, or rather

---

21 Fowler, *To See the Kingdom*, 196.
22 Niebuhr, "Responsibility and Christ," in *Responsible Self,* 167.
23 Niebuhr, *Responsible Self,* 60.

because self-centered power is being wrenched out of our hands? Are we being persecuted, or simply losing privileges?

At any event, enough has been said in this chapter to indicate that God's way with the world, and our way following God, is not one of dictatorial control or brute-force mastery over others and the rest of creation. It is instead the way of responsibility as response-ability. We have tasted a few scriptural texts to that end. Now it is time to delve more deeply and comprehensively into Scripture and its framing. In modern Christendom, the Bible has often been perceived as an encyclopedic answer book. Yet if we are fundamentally responding and responsible creatures, we might better agree with Jacques Ellul that the Bible "is not a recipe book or an answer book, but the opposite: it is the book of questions God asks us."[24] And for Christians or potential Christians, the crucial question it asks us is one posed pointedly by Jesus, about Jesus: "Who do you say that I am?" (Mark 8:29). Framing the Bible as most basically an interrogative book, we may ourselves ask, What are the most pertinent questions it puts to us in a time and space of waning Christendom? And we may, I suggest, find it in certain significant ways to be more relevant and alive than it has been for some nineteen hundred years, since the inception of Christendom.

---

24 Jacques Ellul, *In Season, Out of Season: An Introduction to the Thought of Jacques Ellul* (New York: Harper and Row, 1982), 73.

CHAPTER THREE

The Bible's Renewed Relevance

To be sure, the Bible, theologically interpreted and unified, is always relevant. After all, its story universally spans all of history, from the world's creation to its consummation, still yet to come. It purports to present reality as it really is, including all good and evil, all weal and woe. Since its combined narratives and other material portray "the one and only real world, it must in principle embrace the experience of any present age and reader."[1] So people of various and very different nationalities, races, genders, and historical periods have read and found the Bible resonant. In the end, we are not meant to read the Bible into our own claimed and concocted stories, so much as we are meant to read ourselves into and find our place in its grand, all-encompassing story.

Accordingly, when I now suggest the Bible's "renewed relevance," I do not mean to indicate that it had or has somehow lost its pertinence. For as long as it has existed, there have always been faithful (if flawed) readers of Scripture, finding their stories absorbed in the story set forth in this Book of many books. Instead, what I mean to suggest is that in a particular, significant way we are now closer

---

1 Hans W. Frei, *The Eclipse of Biblical Narrative: A Study in Eighteenth and Nineteenth Century Hermeneutics* (New Haven, CT: Yale University Press, 1974), 3.

to the circumstances of the characters of the scriptural narrative than (European and American) Bible readers have been for many centuries.

More specifically, for most of Scripture's expanse, the Jewish and then Christian faithful must and do live out of control. They live under the sway of successive empires. They are not part of nations or other communities that simply, without challenge, direct their own political, cultural, and social affairs. They are variously immigrants, slaves, wanderers in the wilderness, exiles, subjects of what we would now call colonialism, and resident aliens. Certainly they retain agency and are not persons and communities without impact and influence, especially when they most truly and faithfully serve their God, the sole creator and redeemer of the world. But they rarely rule from the top, if they rule at all. They eschew or are at least bereft of overweening military and governmental power. They cannot depend on exorbitant wealth to get others to do their bidding. Their cultural creations—laws, literature, language, art, and so forth—must always jostle with competing cultures for survival and effect.

If this sounds uncannily like the circumstances within our waning Christendom, that is no accident. For it is within waning Christendom that, as Lutheran theologian and ecumenist George Lindbeck comments, we are now "closer to the situation of the first [Christian] centuries than [we've] been in more than a millennium and a half." Lindbeck goes further: "We are now better placed than perhaps ever before to retrieve, critically and repentantly, the heritage in the Hebrew scriptures, apostolic writings, and early tradition."[2]

This is what I mean by the Bible's renewed relevance. What follows is a modest attempt to flesh out the shape and promise of this fresh, and itself sweeping, pertinence.

---

2 George A. Lindbeck, "Confession and Community: An Israel-like View of the Church," in *The Church in a Postliberal Age,* ed. James J. Buckley (Grand Rapids: Eerdmans), 9.

LIVING OUT OF CONTROL IN THE OLD TESTAMENT

We start in pre-archaeological times, perhaps around 2000 BCE, when Abram (later designated Abraham) was called by a mysterious God out of Ur of the Chaldeans. Sojourning in strange lands, Abraham lived by faith and by his wits—sometimes on the edge of ethics, as when, under threat, he passed off spouse Sarah as a sister rather than a wife (Gen 20:1–3). It was this vulnerable, immigrating man, who left the control and stability of home, that God promised to bless with innumerable descendants, and through those descendants to bless the whole world (Gen 12:3; 15:1–6). Even the early steps of this blessing with descendants, however, are riven with uncertainty and occur out of Abraham and Sarah's control. They despair of bearing a child until, improbably, in old age God grants them a son, Isaac.

Eventually Isaac bears a son named Jacob, later to be called Israel, which means "wrestler with God." Here we see glimmers of the nature and character of the God introduced in our chapter 2, a God who holds power in reserve and dares human beings to confront and grapple with the divine. From Jacob/Israel's loins come most directly what later will be known as the people Israel. Famously, one of Jacob's sons (Joseph) ends up in Egypt as a slave. Through a series of circumstances, Joseph rises to considerable power within Egypt. From this position, he is later able to save his beseeching father and brothers from starvation, whence the nascent Israelites immigrate to Egypt.

All too soon, the immigrants become slaves, and eventually they are subjected to cruel measures, including infanticide and a most onerous labor. Once again, and now perhaps supremely, they live out of control, unable to protect their children and direct their own destinies. After some four hundred years of slavery, God hears their cries for liberation, and sends them Moses and Aaron. God fights early Israel's war of liberation for them. Against Egypt's horses and chariots—the heavy and advanced artillery of the day—the Israelites are defenseless, but God banks the waters of the Red Sea into gigantic walls and lets the Israelites pass through, only to drown the pursuing Egyptian army as the walls come crashing down.

As if to prepare the Israelites to live out of control, and in relationship and faithful response to their God, Israel wanders in the wilderness for forty years. Along the way, God communicates with Moses on Mount Sinai, granting Israel a kind of constitution for its nationhood, and miraculously provides water, manna, and even meat from the sky. The wilderness is a training ground for a community meant to live out of control, in considerable (but not infantile) dependence on its God.

Moses leads Israel to the brink of the promised land, then dies. Joshua and others take the Israelites into an occupation of Canaan. Here we meet profound theological and ethical questions: now Israel is ostensibly not living out of control so much as seeking to control, vanquish, and even exterminate others. The violence and coercion appear clear, abundant, and undeniable. Early on, the church father Origen of Alexandria (c. 185–c. 254) struggled with the book of Joshua and how it fit in the rest of the biblical canon. Origen spiritualized the conquest of Canaan, reading it as the struggle of each soul to root out evil, under the peaceable empowerment of Jesus. Others have since argued that even here, in accounts of physical war, God is depicted as fighting Israel's battles, as with Joshua's symbolic encirclement of Jericho and God's toppling of its walls at the sound of trumpets.[3]

For some four centuries, the Israelites live without a king, under a system of charismatically called judges. Eventually, wishing for more direct control over their national circumstances, the Israelites hanker for a king, so that they may be like other, more self-determining nations. As 1 Samuel reports, God is not pleased by the yearning for

---

3 Ellen F. Davis, *Opening Israel's Scriptures* (New York: Oxford University Press, 2019), 129–143, offers a masterful brief survey of what she calls Joshua's "un-conquest narrative." For other examples of theological and ethical grappling with these questions, see Hinlicky, *Joshua*; Boyd, *Crucifixion of the Warrior God*; and Fleischer, *Old Testament Case for Nonviolence*. On God fighting Israel's battles, see Lind, *Yahweh Is a Warrior*.

a king over Israel, "for," says God to the judge Samuel, "they have not rejected you, but they have rejected me from being king over them" (8:7). Still, Israel presses for a human king, and reluctantly God acquiesces. Samuel tries one last time to dissuade the Israelites, delivering a speech that warns what such kingship will entail:

> These will be the ways of the king who will reign over you: he will take your sons and appoint them to his chariots and to be his horsemen, and to run before his chariots; he will appoint for himself commanders of thousands and commanders of fifties, and some to plow his ground and to reap his harvest, and to make his implements of war and the equipment of his chariots. He will take your daughters to be perfumers and cooks and bakers. He will take the best of your fields and vineyards and olive orchards and give them to his courtiers. He will take one-tenth of your grain and of your vineyards and give it to his officers and to his courtiers. He will take your male and female slaves, and the best of your cattle and donkeys, and put them to his work. He will take one-tenth of your flocks, and you shall be his slaves. And in that day you will cry out because of your king, whom you have chosen for yourselves; but the LORD will not answer you in that day. (1 Sam 8:11–18)

Despite Samuel's passionate plea (and God's own misgivings), Israel is not dissuaded. And so begins the Israelites' experimentation with living more fully in control (as they suppose). Within a generation, Israel's experimentation with kingship reaches its high point with the rule of King David, and even here the kingship is marred by David's disastrous adultery with Bathsheba, and civil-war-level dissension within David's family. In the third generation of kingship, with the rule of Solomon, much of what God and Samuel warns against comes to pass. Solomon sets out to build a great royal complex, and indeed levies much of Israel's wealth and practically enslaves many of its people. After that, for approximately four centuries, the royalty experiment is checkered at best.

In response to the failure of most kings, the prophets of Israel arise. They look beyond human kings to an eschatological promise of God's perfect rule. As the theologian Christian Collins Winn remarks, "The prophetic turn toward eschatology was driven in part by the profound failure of the Israelite monarchy and its ruling class, who did not live into the vision of justice articulated in the law. Given those failures, the prophets emphasize that the only righteous reign will be *God's* reign, and thus it is God who brings the kingdom."[4] The longing for YHWH as Israel's sole and true king is also thematically reflected in a lengthy series of the so-called royal psalms: e.g., Psalms 2; 18; 20; 21; 45; 72; 29; 101; 110; 132; and 144.

Thus we encounter a strong strain of Old Testament thought and action that is ambivalent at best about Israel's experiment to live more in control than it is with YHWH as its one and only king. The Jewish theologian Jon Levenson comments strikingly on this strain:

> In this theology, Sinai serves as an eternal rebuke to man's arrogant belief that he can govern himself. The state is not coeval with God. Rather, it was born at a particular moment in history and under the judgment of a disappointed God. In a better world, one in which man turns to God with all his heart, it would not exist. Moreover, this antimonarchical stream in Israelite religion served to inhibit a simple identification of the people Israel with the states they evolved. For the theological tradition maintained that Israel had been a people before she was a worldly kingdom, a people to whom laws and even a destiny had already been given. She owes neither to the state. Thus, it is of the utmost significance that the Torah, the law of the theo-polity, was, for all its diversity, always ascribed to Moses and not to David, to the humble mediator of the covenant and not to the regal founder of the dynastic state. . . . Israel was a sacral state before she was

---

4 Christian T. Collins Winn, *Jesus, Jubilee, and the Politics of God's Reign* (Grand Rapids: Eerdmans, 2023), xiv.

a political state, she had her law . . . before she raised up a king, and what is perhaps unparalleled in human history, she survived the destruction of her state and even dispersion into the four corners of the world without the loss of that essential identity conferred at Sinai. She was "a kingdom of priests and a holy people" both before and after she was a kingdom of a more mundane kind.[5]

As Levenson indicates, biblical Israel's existence as an independent monarchy was relatively short-lived—by my calculation, for less than a quarter of its history. The northern kingdom (Israel) fell to the Assyrians circa 722 BCE. The southern kingdom (Judah) was vanquished by the Babylonians in 586 BCE. What followed was exile, then return from exile under the Persians, to Jerusalem and its environs, but as a client state. Then would come control from a succession of conquerors, up to the Greeks and finally the Romans. What Israel knew in this period was a way of life largely out of its control, under superpower empires.

Lastly, we should consider that much of the history even of Israel as an independent national entity was written, compiled, and edited in later times, times of exile or subjugation at home. So scholars indicate, for example, that the composition of Deuteronomy most likely began in the seventh century BCE, during the hegemony of the Assyrian empire. Accordingly, this history of an earlier period bears inflections of Israel living out of control, resisting foreign influences and seeking to follow its God despite a lack of national self-determination. Similarly, the prophetic books exhibit a call for Israel to live out of control, under God's shepherding. For instance, the Isaiah traditions may have been developed between the eighth and fifth centuries BCE, "in resistance to the claims of successive ancient empires." In turn, "This paradigm suggests that life before God requires neither an Israelite monarch nor territorial control but

---

5 Jon D. Levenson, *Sinai and Zion: An Entry into the Jewish Bible* (San Francisco: HarperOne, 1985), 74–75.

that communion with the divine could be recovered within sacred space, within the interstices of empire."[6]

LIVING OUT OF CONTROL IN THE NEW TESTAMENT

In comparison to the Old Testament's history of Israel, which covers millennia and comes under the sway of a complex succession of empires, the New Testament story of living out of control is simple. For the New Testament's entirety, there is one superpower, one overarching rule: Rome. And "The reality of [Roman] empire is that 95 percent of the masses are lorded over by 5 percent of the religious, social, economic, military, and political elite; that the 95 percent are slaves, day laborers, artisans, and peasants, all of whom provide cheap labor and produce goods for consumption by the elite besides paying exorbitant taxes, tributes, and rents to them."[7]

But if the Old Testament has been read always as the story of a political entity, the nation or body-politic of Israel, not so the New Testament. Under the aegis of classical and contemporary liberalism, the New Testament has been individualized and privatized. It has often been taken as a plan for how individual souls might be saved for an etherealized heaven, with politics and earthly entities left to their own sorry devices. So the famous statement of evangelist Dwight L. Moody (1837–1899): "I look on this world as a wrecked vessel. God has given me a lifeboat and said to me, 'Moody, save all you can.' God will come in judgment and burn up this world, but the children of God don't belong to this world; they are in it, but not of it, like a ship in the water—Christ will save His Church, but He will save them finally by taking them out of the world."[8]

---

6 See Mark G. Brett, *Locations of God: Political Theology in the Hebrew Bible* (New York: Oxford University Press, 2019), at, respectively, xvii, 86, and 55.

7 Amos Yong, *In the Days of Caesar: Pentecostalism and Political Theology* (Grand Rapids: Eerdmans, 2010), 44.

8 Quoted in J. Christiaan Beker, *Paul the Apostle: The Triumph of God in Life and Thought* (Philadelphia: Fortress, 1980), 371n15.

But if the New Testament church had understood its gospel as individualized and privatized, it had a readily available option, one that would have left it much more comfortable in the Roman orbit. It could have sued, so to speak, for mystery cult status, protesting that it was simply a private club whose individual members presented no challenge to Caesar and his rule. Of course, it very much did not do so. Instead, and immersed in its this-worldly Jewish patrimony, the church conceived of its mission as the "universal restoration" of all creation (Acts 3:21), eventuating in a new heaven and a new earth (Rev 21). The New Testament church, quite like the Judean faith from which it sprang, saw the God of Israel as the Creator-Redeemer of all that is, spanning the world. It looked for a Messiah, a world-changing figure appointed by God to bring justice to earth and rectify all wrongs. Where it differed from its then-fellow Jews was in its conviction that the Messiah had come in the person of the Jew Jesus of Nazareth (Acts 2:36).

Consequently the faith and practice of the New Testament church was through and through political. Jesus was seen as a political threat from the start (consider Herod's massacre of the innocents shortly following his birth) to the end (with his Roman imperial state-sanctioned murder under the sign "King of the Jews"). And the vocabulary, grammar, and logic of the early church was consistently and thoroughly political.

Stay for a moment with the very term and concept of a Messiah, meaning literally "the Anointed One." In the ancient world, including that of Rome, a ruler had oil poured over his head to signal the sacred appointment and approval of his rule. Emperors were anointed ones. Significantly, directly before his crucifixion, Jesus was anointed—and that by a woman (Mark 14:3–9).[9] The anointing announced, symbolically and performatively, Jesus's status as a king—in context, as *the* King.

---

9 On the audacity of the anointing woman and the political ramifications of this episode, see Richard Bauckham, *Jesus and the Eyewitnesses: The Gospels as Eyewitness Testimony* (Grand Rapids: Eerdmans, 2017), 189–194.

Consider next other names applied to Jesus. He is repeatedly called Savior. This, too, was a term applied to Caesar—before and after Jesus's lifetime. Jesus is called *Kyrios,* Lord. We possess today inscriptions of emperors such as Nero bearing the legend "Nero the *kyrios* of the world." Jesus is also called the Son of God, another honorary epithet applied to the emperor, as in coins proclaiming "Tiberius Caesar, son of the divine Augustus."[10] In short, the Roman emperors, in a way quite analogous to Jesus, were considered the ultimate providers of peace, security, protection, health, and sustenance. Further, "the origins of the emperors were often traced to divine sources and heralded by auspicious events including the divine impregnation of human mothers," just as Jesus was believed to be born of a virgin birth.[11] Yet further, an emperor's celebrated arrival at a visited city was known as a *parousia,* just as Jesus's expected second coming was designated.

We might next take up *ekklesia,* the church's name for itself. This meant a called-out body appointed to handle the common affairs— the politics—of a community. It would not be amiss to translate *ekklesia*/church as the "town meeting" or "congress" of God. And the church's mission is to proclaim and embody the promise of the gospel, in New Testament Greek, the *euangelion,* from which we derive our word "evangel." In the Roman world, the *euangelion* designated the good news of events such as the birth of a successor to the emperor, or a victory in a battle fought on his behalf.

Finally, and of momentous importance, Jesus said that he came to bring the *basileia* or kingdom of God, "on earth . . . as it is in heaven" (Matt 6:10). The kingdom of God is of course an enormous concept and reality. But the least we can say of it is that a kingdom is a political entity. To be true to God's kingdom, begun and proleptically accomplished in the life and ministry of Jesus, is minimally to pay attention to the ways in which that kingdom addresses and transforms not simply our individual but our common, communally

---

10 See James W. Thompson, *Christ and Culture in the New Testament* (Eugene, OR: Cascade, 2023), 90n26, 44.

11 Yong, *In the Days of Caesar,* 103.

expressed lives. The kingdom of God is bigger than and precedes and exceeds the church. The church does not bring in the kingdom of God, but it announces the evangel or good news that the world-encompassing kingdom has come. In short, it is not the church's role or place to save the world—that Jesus and his kingdom come has done, unmasking and exposing the powers and principalities in their nakedness and ultimate impotence (Col 2:15). The church is the community now living in light of the kingdom Jesus initiated, proclaiming to the world by deed and word that salvation, full healing, and rectification of all injustice, has arrived.

To understand the politics of Jesus, and the politics of the church derivative from them, we must appreciate an (to use another political word) *inaugurated* eschatology. In his life, death, and resurrection, Jesus the Anointed One has inaugurated or introduced the kingdom. But it will not come in its fullness, its consummation, until Jesus returns. In this regard we must learn to live out of control. Remember, "[T]he task of the church is not to change the world, but to witness to the fact the world has already definitively been changed in the life, death, and resurrection of Jesus Christ."[12] To live out of control, in the words of American theologian Stanley Hauerwas, "means Christians must find the means to make clear to both the oppressed and the oppressor that the cross determines the meaning of history."[13]

We are to be in the world but not of it (John 17:14–15). This does not mean we are without a Christian politics in the world, but that our politics are not those *characteristic* of a broken world. As the Canadian theologian Douglas Harink says, Jesus "did not refuse politics; rather, he proposed a *political alternative* to the way the Romans ruled, and to the way his Judean compatriots hoped to rule when the Messiah came. . . . He called Israel even under occupation and

---

12 Robert J. Dean, *For the Life of the World: Jesus Christ and the Church in the Theologies of Dietrich Bonhoeffer and Stanley Hauerwas* (Eugene, OR: Cascade, 2016), 12.

13 Stanley Hauerwas, "A Story-Formed Community: Reflections on *Watership Down*," in *A Community of Character: Toward a Constructive Christian Social Ethic* (Notre Dame, IN: University of Notre Dame Press, 2981), 11.

oppression to become the *true political community of justice,* a people chosen, ruled, and sustained by God and God's Messiah, their just King. In fact, he claimed, they could be this community of justice without controlling their national territory, security, or destiny."[14]

Jesus came loving and healing neighbors and even his enemies. He served and called his followers to be servants of one another and the world (John 13). He emptied himself of divine prerogatives and called his followers likewise to set aside privileges for the sake of others (Phil 2:1–11). He sided with the oppressed and the poor but offered salvation to the oppressor and the rich as well. Finally, he died vulnerably on a shameful cross to accomplish God's ultimate redemption of the world. In sum, he lived and died out of overweening control so that we might *live.* All this represents the alternative politics of Jesus. To cite Harink again, the life, death, and resurrection of Jesus Christ present a "gift of justice" that "overwhelms the idea that justice is done in human history through coercive power, judgment, condemnation, punishment, and death. Jesus' own justice proceeds from divine abundance and is given abundantly to all. This Sovereign gives rather than takes; he liberates rather than enslaves; he bestows life rather than threatens death."[15]

If we follow in the way of this Jesus, in the power of the Holy Spirit, then, to continue with Harink, "it is *not* our task to grab the levers of history to make it come out right, or to get justice done in the world by controlling events and ruling over other people." Indeed, "We must not imagine the Spirit a divine strength to do what we naturally set our minds to do to gain control. God's power in the Messiah and the Spirit accomplishes justice in those who have learned to *crucify control* and wait on God to complete their work of justice (as God raised Jesus from the dead)."[16] To put it otherwise, and hearkening back to the character of God we explored in chapter 2, we can heed the words of Lutheran theologian Jason Mahn:

14 Douglas Harink, *Resurrecting Justice: Reading Romans for the Life of the World* (Downers Grove, IL: IVP Academic, 2020), 5.

15 Harink, *Resurrecting Justice,* 78.

16 Harink, *Resurrecting Justice,* 117.

"[T]he distinctive nature of God's power is found (without recourse or reserve) in totally vulnerable, self-giving love. God has no power other than the power of love. Any other so-called power—the power to control, to manipulate, or force—is not the power, real power, of vulnerable love."[17]

THE PERVASIVENESS OF POLITICS

Clearly a politics based on the real power of vulnerable love is not the typical politics of our world. In fact, there is a temptation to eschew it as politics at all. Some want to define politics narrowly as what we call "state," "government," or "electoral" politics. These are politics ultimately based on what is considered the justified, monopolistic use of power (including lethal violence) to create, implement, and enforce laws. Certainly this is a form of politics, but in expanse of history it has been understood as only one form of politics.

The Greeks and Romans, and the early Christians among them, pictured politics more broadly, as all in the "realm of life where people pursue[d] temporal goods in common and work[ed] together to ensure a temporal peace. The institutions of government [could] facilitate that temporal peace, but politics [was] not reduced to its institutions or procedures."[18] In this broader sense, "politics" refers to "the relational practices through which a common world of meaning and action is created." It is "about forming, norming, and sustaining a common life"—not only on the national level but the local level (and all in between the two). It is about "how to handle and distribute power constructively."[19] Thus politics occurs and is essential wherever groups and especially communities work together to pursue a shared good and purpose. It occurs wherever power—which we can

---

17 Mahn, *Becoming a Christian in Christendom*, 275.

18 Michael Lamb, *A Commonwealth of Hope: Augustine's Political Thought* (Princeton, NJ: Princeton University Press, 2022), 176.

19 Luke Bretherton, *Christ and the Common Life: Political Theology and the Case for Democracy* (Grand Rapids: Eerdmans, 2019), 34, 36, 2.

here define simply as the capacity to effect or prevent change—is in play. So there are inevitably politics at work within not just designated governmental institutions, but families, corporations and small businesses, clubs and all sorts of associations, and, yes, within the church. (It is not for nothing that we speak of various church "polities"—episcopal, presbyterian, congregational, and so forth.)

Put differently, any community, inasmuch as its identity is defined by its aims or pursuits, and inasmuch as its ethos or character and ethics is defined by the same, works out its identity and ethos through ongoing political acts and practices. Part of what I have tried to suggest in this chapter is that the New Testament church saw and experienced itself as an alternative community, necessarily leaning on and operating out of an alternative politics.[20] It never imagined or worried about taking over the Roman empire. It chose instead to, in that sense, live out of control.

Accordingly, the early Christians saw the church as the primary—though not the sole—political community they belonged to. They concentrated on living in light of the politics of Jesus, which meant sharing power, looking out for one another, and witnessing in manifold ways by their life together that the kingdom of God had come in the ministry, death, and resurrection of Christ, and would arrive at its fullness upon his return. All of this is but to say that the church practiced what has come to be called prefigurative politics. About this, more cries to be said.

---

20 New Testament scholar James Thompson summarizes this globally of the earliest church: "*All* the witnesses of the New Testament describe an alternative society with its own identity and ethos." Thompson, *Christ and Culture in the New Testament,* 183, emphasis added.

CHAPTER FOUR

Prefigurative Politics and Secularity

Prefigurative politics—which I will define shortly—are at least as old as Exodus 19. Some three months after their escape from Egypt, the Israelites arrive at the wilderness of Sinai. God calls Moses to the top of the mountain and there addresses him.

> Thus you shall say to the house of Jacob, and tell the Israelites: You have seen what I did to the Egyptians, and how I bore you on eagles' wings and brought you to myself. Now therefore, if you obey my voice and keep my covenant, you shall be my treasured possession out of all the peoples. Indeed, the whole earth is mine, but you shall be for me a priestly kingdom and a holy nation. These are the words that you shall speak to the Israelites. (Exod 19:3b–6)

Although the whole earth is God's, God calls out and sets apart Israel. Notice that God's address through Moses is meant for Israel as a social unit. Throughout the words are directed to a corporate plural: God has borne the people, not any one individual, on eagle's wings; the "you" that is to obey God's voice and keep God's covenant is plural; it is the solidarity that is Israel that will be a priestly kingdom and a holy nation. Later the prophet Isaiah will designate this people, as a social solidarity, "a light to the nations" (Isa 42:6;

49:6). Along these lines, the Jewish political scientist Gordon Lafer helpfully comments, "The example that Jewish law seeks to set out is one aimed not at individuals but specifically at other 'nations.' . . . This, then, is the universalist mission of Judaism: not to be 'a light unto all individuals,' . . . but rather to teach specific nations how to live *as* a nation."[1]

Israel is a priestly kingdom. Priests mediate the ways of God to humanity and humanity's needs, hopes, and dreams, to God. And Israel is a holy nation, a sacred or set-apart people. Through its roles as a priestly kingdom and a holy nation, Israel will represent God to humanity and humanity to God. When the nations (the gentiles, in biblical language) wonder what the one true God expects of them and desires for them, they can look first and foremost to the example of Israel and God's ways with this uniquely chosen nation.

Drawing directly on the Exodus text, the author of 1 Peter assigns a similar role to the church: "But you are a chosen race, a royal priesthood, a holy nation, God's own people, in order that you may proclaim the mighty acts of him who called you out of darkness into his marvelous light" (2:9–10). The church does not replace Israel but is analogously drawn into a mission like Israel's, witnessing to the same God and that God's eventual redemption of the world. And like Israel, the church is meant to witness as a social unit, a solidarity expected to proclaim in word and deed "the mighty acts of him who called you out of darkness into his marvelous light." Accordingly, the church has been designated variously over time as a "vanguard" or "beachhead" of the kingdom of God in the world. It has been called a "demonstration plot," a "sign and foretaste," a "prototype," and "something of a rough draft of what God intends for all human sociability and interaction."[2]

---

1 Gordon Lafer, "Universalism and Particularism in Jewish Law: Making Sense of Political Loyalties," in *Jewish Identity,* ed. David Theo Goldberg and Michael Krausz (Philadelphia: Temple University Press, 1993), 196.

2 Michael L. Budde, *Foolishness to Gentiles: Essays on Empire, Nationalism, and Discipleship* (Eugene, OR: Cascade, 2022), 82.

Remember what we have previously said about inaugurated eschatology. In Christ, the kingdom of God has come, is present on earth, although it will not come in its fullness, its consummation, until Christ returns. *Here and now*, then, the church is to live in light of that inaugurated kingdom. Like Israel, the church does this through its life together. At its Eucharist, it foreshadows and represents the great banquet that will occur at time's end, when "people will come from east and west, from north and south, and will eat in the kingdom of God" (Luke 13:29; cf. Matt 8:11). In its inclusion of all races, genders, and social castes (Gal 3:28), the church represents the unity and equality of every person in God. In its practices of forgiveness and justice, it is a token of how people may be reconciled and saved from estrangement. The church, in short, is an eschatological people through and through, and it may rightly be said that all its ethics is "lived eschatology."[3]

To be sure, the church often fails and even actively violates its high calling. Soberingly, we are reminded that judgment begins with the house of the Lord (1 Pet 4:17). God save us from coming to God "for solace only, and not for strength; for pardon only, and not for renewal."[4] Yet, to the extent we recover our calling, even our failures may be sources or models of a faithful politics. As political scientist Michael Budde remarks, "The Church does not cause the Kingdom to advance, but it is meant to show the world what human community starts to look like as the Kingdom becomes a lived reality." It does this not only by noble example but "in and through its sins, mistakes, wrong turns, and reversals—it does this through showing what penance and reconciliation can make possible, by showing that the past need not have a death-grip on the present and future, and by imitating however it can the self-giving love of God toward one another and those outside its community."[5] Consequently, in both its

---

3 J. Richard Middleton, *A New Heaven and a New Earth: Reclaiming Biblical Eschatology* (Grand Rapids: Baker Academic, 2014), 24.

4 Book of Common Prayer, Eucharistic Prayer C, 372.

5 Budde, *Foolishness to Gentiles*, 86.

successes and its failures, the church today may prefigure the world as it will be tomorrow, at the eschaton.

DEFINITIONS AND EXAMPLES

Though prefigurative politics in practice have existed for centuries, they were not named as such until the 1970s. Then secular theorist Carl Boggs defined prefigurative politics as an organization or movement embodying "those forms of social relations, decision-making, culture, and human experience that are [its] ultimate goal."[6] For instance, an organization with feminist goals would contradict itself and confute its aims if it was patriarchally structured. Likewise, a movement seeking to rid the world of war (or at least lessen its occurrence) would need to develop ways of making decisions and promoting its aims that were themselves nonviolent. Boggs and other theorists and activists hearkened to Mahatma Gandhi's alleged aphorism, "Be the change that you wish to see in the world."[7] (Centuries earlier, Augustine of Hippo preached to his church, "You are hoping for the good; be what you hope for.")[8]

The theorist-activists Paul Raekstad and Sofa Saio Gradin define prefigurative politics a bit more broadly than Boggs. For them, prefigurative politics involves "the deliberate experimental implementation of desired future social relations and practices in the here-and-now." Metaphorically, they speak of "planting the seeds of the society of the future in the soil" of today's world. Putting it slightly differently, they say, "Being committed to prefigurative politics means being committed to the idea that if we want to replace certain social structures, then we need to reflect some aspect(s) of the future structures we want in the movements we

---

6 Quoted in Paul Raekstad and Sofa Saio Gradin, *Prefigurative Politics: Building Tomorrow Today* (Cambridge: Polity, 2020), 10.

7 Raekstad and Gradin, *Prefigurative Politics*, 5.

8 Augustine, Sermon 325A.5, cited in Lamb, *A Commonwealth of Hope*, 263.

develop to fight for them." Later they cite proponents of prefigurative politics who remark on "opposing *and* proposing," or of being "against-and-beyond."[9]

I suspect it takes little imagination to see how today's secular prefigurative politics parallel (or echo) the earlier practices of Judaism and Christianity. I need only add that prefigurative politics present a way of doing politics out of control. Such politics need not impose or coerce. Instead, they offer embodiments of ways of living together differently. They then leave these enfleshed, social experiments for others outside the church to reject, or to accept and appropriate. Furthermore, they may arouse the imagination of the watching world, prompting questions and curiosity. In such cases, the church may respond evangelistically, telling the story of Israel and Jesus Christ that has grounded, motivated, and animated the church's prefigurative, eschatological politics. To round out this discussion, let me briefly survey a few examples of Christian prefigurative politics, from history and contemporary times.

An early example comes from the fourth century, when Basil of Caesarea founded the first hospital, in Cappadocia (located in present-day Turkey). The Greeks and Romans had long before made significant contributions to the practice of medicine, but no one had thought to establish organized centers of care for the sick and injured. After Basil's innovation, hospitals spread throughout the East and the West. This Christian heritage is reflected in the names of many modern hospitals: St. Vincent's, St. Luke's, Presbyterian, and so forth. And of course this prefiguration has been adopted by a host of others, based in various faiths.[10]

A second example concerns monastic communities. Launched in the fourth century, monasteries have modeled alternative economies,

---

9 Raekstad and Gradin, *Prefigurative Politics,* respectively at 10 (emphasis deleted), 4, 10, and 38. Consult also the consideration of prefigurative politics in Evan B. Howard, *Deep and Wide: Reflections on Socio-Political Engagement, Monasticism(s), and the Christian Life* (Eugene, OR: Cascade, 2023), 107–109.

10 C. Ben Mitchell, "The Christian Origins of Hospitals," Bible Mesh, https://biblemesh.com/blog/the-christian-origin-of -hospitals/.

preserved books and promoted literacy, practiced hospitality, and done much more besides—and this always with an eye to influencing those in and beyond the church. With influence and visibility in mind, Augustine chose to locate his monastery in the middle of the city rather than a distant, isolated desert.[11] Monasticism is a Catholic institution, but in recent decades many Protestant communities have adopted their own form of it, called New Monasticism. New Monastics include married and single members, and often locate their intentional communities in inner cities. Like their forerunners in traditional monasticism, the New Monastics have majored in hospitality and rejuvenation of neighborhoods. In addition, they have enacted prophetic and dramatic demonstrations, such as literally beating disused guns into plowshares.[12]

Raekstad and Gradin note a third example. "North American sections of the modern Global Justice Movement seem mostly to have got their ideas about consensus decision-making from post-war feminist and anti-nuclear movements, who were in turn influenced by Quaker practices."[13] The Quakers, meanwhile, developed their consensus decision-making by turning to the biblical book of Acts. They looked especially to Acts 15 and the early deliberations of the so-called Council at Jerusalem.

Lastly, I point to the restorative justice movement. Founded by Canadian Mennonites in the 1970s, this movement seeks to facilitate dialogue between the victims and perpetrators of crimes. Drawing on the biblical motif of shalom, or peace and wholeness, as well as listening practices honed by indigenous peoples such as the Maori of New Zealand, facilitators in the restorative justice movement have intervened in everything from minor crimes like vandalism, all the way through to horrifically violent crimes including rape and murder. No perpetrators—let alone victims—are forced into

---

11 Lamb, *Commonwealth of Hope*, 213.

12 See Shane Claiborne and Michael Martin, *Beating Guns: Hope for People Who Are Weary of Violence* (Grand Rapids: Brazos, 2019).

13 Raekstad and Gradin, *Prefigurative Politics*, 65.

these processes, but in countless cases those who sought participation have been helped to achieve real measures of healing and reconciliation.[14]

THE CHRISTIAN CASE FOR SECULARITY

I take it that prefigurative politics are the central and primary politics of the church and Christians. We should always be on the lookout for opportunities to enact imaginative possibilities that point to the kingdom of God come and coming in Christ. Christians of all sorts—whether they are professional politicians or even exercise the right to vote—can participate in prefigurative politics. But of course we may wonder about the Christian role particularly in governmental or elective politics. How should Christians relate to the rough and tumble of local, state, and national governmental politics? To put the question more pointedly, how should the church and Christians respond to governmental political endeavors in a time and place of secular rule?

An answer begins with what may be a surprising realization: secularity is a Christian invention. The great Augustine of Hippo (354–430), who wrote prolifically on Christian politics of all kinds, employed the term *saeculum* (from which we derive the term "secular") to name the time between Christ's inauguration of the kingdom of God and its consummation at the end of history. We now use mainly spatial metaphors to describe secularity or secularism. For instance, we talk about living "under the secular regime." Or we imagine that Christian politics occur "over here," with Christian actors, and secular politics "over there," with secular actors—such as those nasty secular humanists. To be truer to Augustine, we should not lean on spatial metaphors, but on metaphors that are temporal, or immersed in time and the passage of history. Secularity is the time between the times—between Christ's first advent and the eschaton.

---

14 This thumbnail sketch of the restorative justice movement draws on personal conversations with practitioner Ted Lewis, July 12 and 13, 2023.

In Augustine's terms, secularity is time when the two cities (the city of God and the city of man) are mixed, shoulder by shoulder, jostling against and sometimes interpenetrating one another. Concentrating on the temporal metaphor, theologian Eric Gregory comments, "In this way, the 'secular' contrasts not with the 'sacred' but the 'eternal' . . ."[15]

Paying attention to Augustine, the political theologian Luke Bretherton writes, "The demarcation of the current age as secular is a Christian innovation that breaks open divisions between sacred and profane. If something is secular, it can be both sacred and profane, rather than sacred or profane, concerned with both the immanent and the transcendent, able to participate simultaneously is the penultimate and the ultimate. Secular time is thereby ambiguous and contingent."[16] In the language employed in this book, secularity is the time in which Christians live out of control. We live in a time when the kingdom of God has not come in its fullness, when no church or governmental regime can be simply or wholly identified with the kingdom; when, for our (and others') temporal good, we have to live responsibly with people of many other faiths and no declared faith tradition at all. For example, vehicle regulation and traffic infrastructure serve people of all persuasions; without them, commerce and modern travel of any sort would grind to a halt. Or we may think of sex trafficking—governmental politics that effectively curb it should be urgently appealing to all people of good will, or simply minimal human decency. In the time between the times, the *saeculum*, there are innumerable instances where the Christians should and must live responsibly with their fellow citizens who do not share their faith convictions. In this sense, secularity should not be feared but embraced.

Of course, there is another sense in which secularism (the ideology) may be objectionable. Since roughly the eighteenth century, secularism and secularization theory have touted the decline of

---

15 Quoted in Lamb, *Commonwealth of Hope*, 175.
16 Bretherton, *Christ and the Common Life*, 231.

traditional faith. Bretherton summarizes it this way: "In the process the temporality of the secular shifts from a nonlinear, christological conception (all times are equidistant from Christ, who is the origin, the center, and the end [goal] of history) to a linear and progressive temporality (all time is inexorably moving forward, finding its apogee in a religion-free modernity)."[17] In other words, Augustine's secularity morphs into an ideology that supposes all religion is bad, or should at least be strictly privatized and kept out of the public square. No wonder Christians blanch at this sort of secularity.

The eminent Anglican theologian Rowan Williams here intervenes with a crucial distinction, between "programmatic" and "procedural" secularism. "Programmatic secularism is something more like what is often seen (not always accurately) as the French paradigm, in which any and every public manifestation of any particular religious allegiance is to be ironed out so that everyone may share a clear public loyalty to the state unclouded by 'private' convictions, and any signs of such 'private' convictions are rigorously banned from public space."[18] In the American context, the wall of separation between church and state is then interpreted maximally: no Christian (or other religious) convictions should be given voice in the public square.

Procedural secularism, by contrast, is "a public policy which declines to give advantage or preference to any one religious body over others."[19] At the same time, Christians and others may be allowed to speak and advocate from their convictions, which ground, motivate, and animate all important aspects of their lives. "So," says Williams, "it is possible to imagine a 'procedurally' secular society and legal system which is always open to being persuaded by confessional or ideological argument on particular issues, but is not committed to privileging permanently any one confessional

---

17 Bretherton, *Christ and the Common Life*, 232.

18 Rowan Williams, *Faith in the Public Square* (London: Continuum, 2012), 2–3. I have added scare quotes around the word *private*.

19 Williams, *Faith in the Public Square*, 2.

group."[20] In sum, procedural secularism, "as a characteristic of the public domain, means that there is not legal privilege for any specific religious position; but not that such positions are regarded as simply private convictions."[21]

For Christians properly prepared to live out of control, procedural secularism presents no problem. Such Christians do not expect the government to privilege the church, to make it the always-determining voice in public debate. At the same time, Christians living out of control do not want to forfeit their deepest convictions, which concern nothing less than the salvation of the world, or to lose all agency and effect in the sphere of governmental politics. To live eschatologically, in the time between the times otherwise known as secularity, is to accept responsibility to live on an open and level playing field with all other people, who are also immersed in the *saeculum*.

Given an Augustinian understanding of secularity and Williams's crucial distinction between programmatic and procedural secularism, we can see better what has actually transpired since the French Revolution and later attempts to erase religion from the public square. Traditional faith has not died off. Secular "faiths"—from Nazism to Soviet communism—have not resulted in a perfect world. As Bretherton puts it eloquently, "It turns out that the modern world is like a Jacuzzi in which belief and unbelief are bubbling up from everywhere and contesting each other in a dynamic, constantly changing, and not very hygienic environment. . . . No one, from the confessional Darwinist to the so-called fundamentalist, can assume his or her view is 'normal' or simply the way things will be." What results is the "mutual fragilization" of all beliefs and practices, whether "skeptical" or "religious."[22]

So what we have to deal with is not secularism in the inimical sense but plurality. Our late modern world is highly pluralistic, in

20 Williams, *Faith in the Public Square*, 28.
21 Williams, *Faith in the Public Square*, 20.
22 Bretherton, *Christ and the Common Life*, 249.

terms of ideologies, religions, cultures, political programs, economic systems, and so forth. In chapter 3, I recounted several regards in which today's world more nearly reflects, for the first time in nearly two millennia, the world of the New Testament church. Here, with pluralism, is yet another. In the ancient Mediterranean world, Jews and Christians encountered statuary honoring foreign gods on almost every street corner. Meals routinely featured libations poured to the Roman emperor, considered a god on earth. Nearly every artistic performance featured and/or paid homage to Greek and Roman deities.[23] Accordingly, pluralism was no stranger to the earliest church, which lived out of control in its midst.

Today's church, to the extent it is willing to live out of control, can coexist with and in many regards honor pluralism and secularity. They are congruent with a God who makes room for human freedom and is not fundamentally about coercion of God's creation. They are fitting in the time between the times, also known as the *saeculum*. They necessitate and encourage a real degree of humility, of the recognition that Christians are not always right and frequently have much to learn from those outside the church. (And humility, after all, is a premier Christian virtue.) Finally, they require patience, the same sort of patience with a messy world exercised by our longsuffering and merciful God. As the Anglican theologian Oliver O'Donovan puts it, "Secularity is a stance of patience in the face of plurality, made sense of by eschatological hope."[24] Seen through a Christian eschatological lens, secularity and pluralism should not tempt despair but spark hope, encourage faith, and, alongside prefigurative politics, position the church to most fulsomely witness to the God of Israel met in Jesus Christ.

---

23 For more on the pluralism of the ancient world, and its parallels with our own hyperpluralistic environment, see my *Naming Neoliberalism: Exposing the Spirit of Our Age* (Minneapolis: Fortress, 2021), 193–194.

24 Cited in Lamb, *Commonwealth of Hope,* 358n71.

CHAPTER FIVE

Christian Nationalism

An Alternative to Living Out of Control

This book is dedicated to telling a viable and compelling story of how Christians may live out of control. That story will resume with the next chapter. At this point, however, nearly halfway through the book, it behooves us to pay some sustained attention to an alternative story, a story of Christians regaining control of (at least) the American polity and culture. The most prominent such story in our time is that of Christian nationalism.

According to some estimates, nearly 52 percent of Americans either fully embrace or lean toward Christian nationalism. Some 55 percent of those who fully embrace it identify as evangelicals. Half of the true believers live in the South, and 70 percent are white. Among those who lean toward, but do not fully embrace, Christian nationalism, one-third live in the South, another one-third in the Midwest, and two-thirds are white.[1]

It is not hard to find churches devoted to Christian nationalism. Such churches are often militaristic in their appeal. Journalist Jeff Sharlet visited the Church of Glad Tidings, in Yuba

---

1 See Andrew L. Whitehead and Samuel L. Perry, *Taking America Back for God: Christian Nationalism in the United States* (New York: Oxford University Press, 2020), 25, 34, 37, 39.

City, California. There he found a pulpit fashioned of swords. He watched as General Michael Flynn, Donald Trump's first national security advisor, was called to the stage and gifted with a customized AR-15. He noticed there were no crosses in the church. Upon inquiry, Sharlet writes, Pastor Dave Bryan "compared the cross, the crucifix, the method by which Jesus is believed, by those who believe, to have died for our sins, to the tender dove: weak-tea figuration that fails to convey the great breadth of ass kicked by Christ once he was risen."[2]

I might fill this chapter with such anecdotes. I choose instead to shift the gaze to the most serious contemporary exposition of Christian nationalism I am aware of, Stephen Wolfe's *The Case for Christian Nationalism*.[3] Unlike the declarations of popular proponents of Christian nationalism, such as the politicians Marjorie Taylor Greene and Tommy Tuberville, Wolfe's advocacy is neither coy nor confused. Educated at Louisiana State University and Princeton, Wolfe argues full throatily and with no holds barred. He is also intelligent, informed, and rigorously coherent. In addition, Wolfe's book comes with commendations by other serious thinkers of a nationalist bent. Yoram Hazony, the Israeli nationalistic conservative of note, calls it "a pioneering work that paves the way for a new genre of American Christian-nationalist political theory." And R. R. Reno, editor of *First Things*, the elite journal of religion and public affairs, enthuses, "Clearly argued and forceful in its conclusions, *The Case for Christian Nationalism* sets the standard for today's debates."[4] So what is Wolfe's alternative to the church living out of control?

---

2 Jeff Sharlet, *The Undertow: Scenes from a Slow Civil War* (New York: W. W. Norton, 2023), 173–74.

3 Stephen Wolfe, *The Case for Christian Nationalism* (Moscow, ID: Canon, 2022). Hereafter, page number references to this book will be cited parenthetically within the text. Unless otherwise indicated, I have preserved Wolfe's italicized emphases.

4 Both endorsements are found on the Amazon.com page for Wolfe's book.

THE INTENDED READERSHIP

Stephen Wolfe straightforwardly declares the intended main readership of his book. He tells us he is "speaking largely to a Western European male audience" (119). He is not bashful about his patriarchal presuppositions. "[T]he man governs the household, orienting it to the divine mission *he* received from God, which *he* is responsible to see fulfilled. The wife is the necessary support for the man as he meets his obligations to civil community and the broader mission of humanity" (57–58). And "the public signaling of political interest (whether through voting or other mechanisms) would be conducted by men, for they represent their households and everyone in it" (73). This seems to throw female suffrage into question, but at another place Wolfe admits that on account of the fall "natural hierarchical power is now abused," so that there must be some checks on it. And these checks might include "free, frequent, and regular elections and other egalitarian institutions, such as universal suffrage, civil rights, and anti-discrimination labor laws" (90). Even here, though, he is quick to note that such "egalitarian" norms "are not purely natural to humankind" (90). Meanwhile, "Whether or not unmarried people (both men and women) and widows (in a fallen world) can participate [in voting and other political processes] is a matter of prudence and subject to the determination of each community" (73n60).

Beyond this, in terms of intended readership, Wolfe informs us that he writes from a Reformed, and specifically Presbyterian, point of view. He draws "mainly from the 16th and 17th centuries, in which Reformed theology was very Thomistic and catholic" (17). He notes that he here uses "catholic" as the Reformers did, "referring to the fundamental articles of faith taught by and since the Church Fathers" (18n15). Though his account is "more Presbyterian in form," Wolfe hopes it will appeal to Anglicans and Lutherans as well and not least (9n12).

Further still, we may deduce aspects of Wolfe's readership from his rhetoric. "I fully acknowledge that my goal is to reinvigorate Christendom in the West—that is my chief aim. The question for most of my audience is, 'Which way, Western Man—the suicide of the West or its revitalization?'" (119). For Wolfe and the readers most likely to find him convincing, then, the stakes are supremely high and represent a black-and-white either/or: either the Christendom-led resurrection of the West, or its death by cultural suicide. They may also be folk who do not much like America—at least as it now exists. It is an America in which the "straight white male" is supposedly "the chief out-group" (436), in which abhorrent practices or beliefs now include "feminism, homosexuality, gender fluidity, secularism, porn, and base entertainment" (439), in which regular, good folk are overrun by a "ruling class" that "is an occupying force" (441), which has, among other things, "forced homosexual marriage on all states" as nothing less than "an imperial imposition" (443). It is, not least, an America ruled by women—a "gynocracy" wherein "The most insane and damaging sociological trends of our modern society are female-driven" (451). In addition, it should be noted that Wolfe excoriates the federal government and appeals to states' rights (473–474). Admittedly, most of this rhetoric comes from Wolfe's epilogue, where he lets down his guard and rants for a spell. Still, it indicates where he is coming from and suggests that his main, immediate appeal is surely to what Yoram Hazony calls "the contemporary dissident right."[5]

NATURAL LAW: THE BASIS OF CHRISTIAN NATIONALISM

Key to understanding Wolfe's case is its reliance, almost exclusively, on natural law. Wolfe writes, "Reformed theologians universally agreed that the natural law was not eliminated at the fall of man, nor was it abolished, superseded, added to, or modified by the Gospel" (50). And: the "Gospel does not eliminate, undermine, or 'critique' the basic principles that have structured societies and relations of all ages and people" (105). One of these "basic principles" is that

---

5 Hazony endorsement, on the Amazon.com page for Wolfe's book.

men should gather and govern themselves in separate communities or nationalities: "If Adam had not fallen, he and his progeny would have multiplied on the earth. They would have formed communities, for no man can live well when alone and when not in combination with others. These communities would have been distinct, or separate nations, because even unfallen man would have had natural limitations and been bounded by geography, arability, and other factors" (21). Accordingly, "the formation of nations is not a product of the fall; it is natural to man as man" (22). Wolfe elaborates:

Since those who share a culture are similar people, and since cultural similarity is necessary for the common good, I argue that the natural inclination to dwell among similar people is good and necessary. Grace does not destroy or "critique" it. Choosing similar people over dissimilar people is not a result of fallenness, but is natural to man as man. Why? Because we are drawn by deep instinct to our good. Indeed, one *ought* to prefer and love more those who are more similar to him, and much good would result in the world if we all preferred our own and minded our own business. (24–25)

For Wolfe, hierarchy is also dictated by natural law. Not only are women to be submissive to men, but a few men should naturally rule most other men. This applies to "bodily stature, beauty, knowledge, virtue, domestic authority, and civil authority" (66). In all such areas, some are "suitable for a position of superiority and others suitable for obedience" (68). In this regard Wolfe approvingly quotes Althusius: "[I]t is inborn to the more powerful and prudent to dominate and rule weaker men, just as it is also considered inborn for inferiors to submit" (73).[6]

Following Christ's advent, natural law is not abrogated or weakened, but supernaturally fulfilled and perfected. Now the strong,

---

6 Johannes Althusius (1563–1638) was a German jurist and Calvinist political philosopher.

naturally superior men who should rule are Christian men. In Christ, the "people of God on earth are a restored humanity. Restored man ought to be naturally drawn to dominion, for domination is the natural end or purpose of these gifts" (23). Again: "To be sure, there is important commonality between the redeemed and the unredeemed, both being human. But restorative grace sets the redeemed apart on earth—constituting a restored humanity on earth—and, on that basis, Christians can and ought to exercise dominion in the name of God" (100; cf. 110). By the same logic, the Christian nation is "the nation perfected. . . . Just as grace clarifies for sinful man his true end and supplies the means to attain it, Christianity completes the nation by ordering law, customs, and social expectations to heavenly life" (174). Indeed, "The Christian nation is the complete image of eternal life on earth" (223) and "A Christian body of law is the only *complete* and *true* body of law" (263).

Wolfe then yearns for a Christian magistrate or "prince" who is "the quintessential great man" (276). A Christian nation need not necessarily be a monarchy, but Wolfe envisions "a measured and theocratic Caesarism—the prince as a world-shaker for our time, who brings Christian people to self-consciousness and who, in his rise, restores their will for their good" (279). The superlatives for the Christian prince breathlessly pile up. He "mediates God's divine civil rule" (286). He "makes public judgments in applications of God's natural law, effectively creating law (though derivative of natural law), and he has the power to bring about what he commands. Thus, the prince holds the most excellent office, exceeding even that of the church minister, for it is most like God" (286). "In a sense, we see God in the magistrate" (287). "Having the highest office on earth, the good prince resembles God to the people. Indeed, he is the closest image of God on earth" (287) He is "the divinely sanctioned vicar of God," "Christ's deputy," and "an image of Christ to his people," nothing less than "a national god" (290, 309, 289).

Rooted in natural law, empowered by grace to a total and "definitive" sanctification (93), and led by a truly awesome prince, Christian nationalism, in sum, "is a totality of national action, consisting of civil laws and social customs, conducted by a Christian nation as a Christian nation, in order to procure for itself both earthly and heavenly good in Christ" (9, italics deleted). On the ground, then, what does this entail?

ENTAILMENTS

Wolfe carefully distinguishes civil law's ambit and remit. They do not include the conscience and matters of the "soul." To wit: "Civil law can direct men only outwardly; it cannot command the soul. The conscience is free from coercion" (31). The "direct object" of legislation cannot be the conscience. "Thus, civil action for the advancement of the Gospel only *indirectly* operates to that end" (182; cf. 79). Still, the reach of this indirectness is considerable, for "external religion" falls under the remit of civil law (34–35). Accordingly, Christian nationalist legislators "can outwardly order people to that which is good for the soul. Thus, Sabbath laws are just, because they remove distractions for holy worship. Laws can also penalize blasphemy and irreverence in the interest of public peace and Christian peoplehood" (31). We can then expect businesses closed on Sunday and legal penalization of "blasphemy and irreverence," however these are defined.

"External religion" includes not only "blasphemy" and "Sabbath-breaking," but also "heretical teaching" and "false rites" (34–35). "Heretical teaching" is not defined; that would be left up to Christian nationalist legislators. But perhaps, among other things, heresy would be a basis to "repudiate neo-Anabaptist attempts to subvert a durable Christian social order" (241). Nor are "false rites" defined, but if, as Wolfe holds, Christianity is the one true and complete religion, and to be legally privileged as such, we can only wonder if Jews, Muslims, Hindus, and other non-Christians would be banned from gathering and worshiping with their rites. In any event, Wolfe explicitly declares that these non-Christians would not be regarded as politically equal in his Christian nation. "Non-Christians living among

us are entitled to justice, peace, and safety, but they are not entitled
to political equality . . ." (346). "The Christian's posture towards the
earth ought to be that it is *ours*, not theirs, for we are co-heirs with
Christ" (346). Christian nationalism will exclude "the political and
social influence of non-Christian religion and its adherents" (385;
cf. 392). Furthermore, in a Christian America, "any non-Christian
American would have to hyphenate their Americanness, symbolizing
their separation from the core of American religious life" (175n2).
Thus, it is hard to see non-Christians as anything but second-class
citizens in Wolfe's declared Christian nation. As for "conforming"
Christians, "Magistrates can require that everyone who is baptized
will attend [worship services], even those who are unconfirmed by
the church and not allowed to participate in the Supper" (396).

Will women be excluded from governmental and church leadership? Wolfe does not say, but we can suspect as much from his
exposition of a male-headed hierarchy and his passionate aversion
to "gynocracy." Wolfe is explicit that the longed-for Christian prince
"should return us to a masculine society, which alone can remedy
the gynocratic contradictions that plague our society" (292). As for
church leadership, we can fairly guess Wolfe wants women to be
subordinated here as he clearly expects them to be in the home. And
as a feature of our national decline, he does derogate "priestesses
[who] now have regular columns in national newspapers" (231).[7]

Proactively, Wolfe's Christian nation would fund theological education and seminaries, church buildings, and ministers' salaries
(182). It would erect public religious displays such as monuments,
"institute special days of religious observance" (318), and incorporate
"religious elements into civil events," for if "civil government cannot
command people to contemplate heavenly things," it "can create the
best outward conditions for such contemplation, which serve as visible reminders of the highest purposes for which man was created"

---

7 Presumably he here has in mind Tish Harrison Warren, a former *New York
Times* columnist who is ordained in the Anglican Church in North America.
Wolfe does not mention the allowability of homosexuals in government or other
leadership, but again his general tenor suggests he would exclude it.

(79). Such direction might get right down to the minutiae of church furniture. "A prince may require the elevation of the pulpit above the Lord's Table in church construction, for example. This follows a natural principle of order, signifying that the dependent element is beneath the thing on which it depends (viz., the preaching of the Word goes before the administration of the Lord's Supper)" (317). Thus would Wolfe's Protestant Christian America legally mandate the reconstruction and rearrangement of most Episcopal churches—not to mention all Roman Catholic churches.

Taken together, these proposals for a Christian nationalism are breathtakingly radical, both wide- and deep-ranging. If their institution is attempted, vigorous opposition, including from many Christians, would be bound to arise. Not only cultural and political but violent conflict might occur. Wolfe does not flinch from the prospect of lethal violence. In fact, he sees Christians of his ilk already under attack and oppression from "secularist captors" (352). The current American "regime" is corrupt and hostile, and Wolfe verges on demonization in describing it as an enemy of the church, "an enemy of the human race, and an enemy of God" (456, 338).

In this context, Wolfe argues that violent resistance and revolution are justifiable. For, "any civil command to do evil or abstain from what is good is not a command of God, nor is it backed by divine power; it is a command of *men*, and no man by his own power can bind another man's conscience to action. To resist such power is not to resist God but to resist tyrannical men" (33). In such circumstances, "A just, violent revolution is a type of defensive war" (33). "National harm can include oppression against true religion, and thus the people can conduct revolution in order to restore true religion" (34). Individuals have a natural right and duty to self-preservation and self-defense in the interest of "their life and goods." So too do nations, "for both are moral entities." And, "Since national self-preservation is a command of God and since the injustice of tyrants harms the nation, violent resistance is morally permissible, for God sufficiently augmented earthly powers to shore up earthly good in response to the fall . . . , and violence is necessary at times to eliminate tyranny and preserve the nation" (337). The requirement for violent resistance and even revolution is tyranny, and Wolfe confesses that tyranny has already befallen "historic Christianity" and the genuine, militant church. He rhetorically asks, "When Christians are under a universalizing and totalizing non-Christian regime that wields implicit powers against true religion, how is this not tyranny?" (345).

Wolfe implicitly recognizes that Christendom has waned, and he seems well aware that Christian nationalism, at least of his sort, is in a minority. Therefore, he leans (at least for the nearer future) less toward sedition, in terms of overthrowing the US federal government, and more toward secession, in terms of a state or states leaving the union to establish a Christian nation. He argues for the possibility of just revolutions and for the propriety of a Christian people requesting (then demanding?) "separation and independence" (328n3). He suggests that backers of a Christian nation appeal to states' powers and "lesser magistrates" who are faithful to his vision. "State governors are deputies of God, not deputies of the federal government, and their power from God is for good, not for evil. Thus, they must resist and nullify unjust and tyrannical laws imposed on the people by the federal government" (473). And: "We should look again to the states. Christian nationalists ought to elect Christians into state office, especially those who are willing to be the lesser magistrate against an unjust federal government" (474).

TAKING MEASURE

For decades, professing conservatives have complained about the "social engineering" efforts of the political left. It's ironic, then, that Christian nationalists, self-styled as conservatives, propose a gargantuan "cultural engineering" project.[8] Further, their grasp of culture and how it works is weak. For one thing, cultures are fuzzy and

---

8 For criticism of "cultural engineering" and Christian nationalism, see Paul D. Miller, *The Religion of American Greatness: What's Wrong with Christian Nationalism* (Downers Grove, IL: IVP Academic, 2022).

permeable. As political scientist Paul Miller, an astute evangelical critic of nationalism, puts it, the map "of the world's culture is not a checkerboard; it is a Venn diagram—and the overlapping circles are blobs of irregular size and shape that fade imperceptibly into one another. . . . Different cultures certainly exist, but the boundaries between them are blurry. Cultures overlap. The nationalist vision depends on being able to draw clear and hard boundaries between cultures." But "that effort is essentially impossible, especially on the ground near the borders where cultures overlap and mingle."[9] In addition, cultures are fluid and constantly changing; what was significantly true of a culture ten years ago may not be today. All of this is especially the case in the highly accelerated, globalized milieu of the twenty-first century. In this light, nationalism, including Christian nationalism, is dangerously nostalgic, pining for "an imagined past of cultural simplicity when everyone supposedly knew who 'we' and who 'they' were, a transplantation of simple tribalism to the era of large, impersonal, geographically extensive states."[10]

Related to tribalism and understandings of culture is the important matter of race. By his own admission, Wolfe's Christian nationalism is deeply rooted in "Western European [i.e., white] male" culture (119). We need to be exceedingly aware of whiteness's ability to become invisible, even (or especially) as it reigns over other races and cultures. As the Christian ethicist David Horrell reminds us, whiteness (with other races) is not an objective or "essential" characteristic. It is rather "a socially constructed, historically contingent, and ideologically loaded category."[11] In a world dominated

---

9 Miller, *Religion of American Greatness*, 63.

10 Miller, *Religion of American Greatness*, 70.

11 David G. Horrell, *Ethnicity and Inclusion: Religion, Race, and Whiteness in Constructions of Jewish and Christian Identities* (Grand Rapids: Eerdmans, 2020), 312. This is demonstrated by considering those who, as recently as the nineteenth and twentieth centuries, were considered "non-white." The category included Italians, the Irish, Greeks, Armenians, Hungarians, Serbians, Slovenians, Poles, Jews, Montenegrins, Croatians, Russians, Bulgarians, Czechs, Slovaks, and Finns. See Budde, *Foolishess to Gentiles*, 53.

by folks of Western European descent, whiteness becomes invisible and is assumed as "universal, unmarked, unraced"— "just people."[12] Of course, it is only invisible to those who inhabit it; to others it is glaring. In response, we need to recognize that whiteness is socially constructed and "particularize" it. As Horrell puts it, "Particularizing whiteness and subjecting it to critical scrutiny is one way to dethrone this perspective from a position of assumed universality and disembodied rationality and to place it alongside—not 'above'— other embodied and particular perspectives."[13]

Wolfe guards against a white supremacist appropriation of his Christian nationalism with but a single (uncharacteristically obscure) footnote, dismissing concerns about the singular whiteness of his case as distracting "people from recognizing and acting for their people-groups, many of which (to be sure) are majority 'white' but are not so on the basis of a modern racialist principle" (119n3). Whatever exactly that means, the susceptibility of Wolfe's views to white supremacist sentiments surfaced when it was learned that Thomas Achord, the cohost of a podcast with Wolfe, supported what Achord called a "robust race realist white nationalism." On Twitter, Achord responded to a post from the American Jewish Committee with "OK jew," referred to representative Cori Bush (of Missouri) as a "Negress," and told the Black evangelical antiracist Jemar Tisby, "Please leave soon.—Sincerely, All White Peoples." As the *New Yorker*'s Kelefa Sanneh commented, the "Achord affair made it clear that even a sympathetic reader of Wolfe's book could be confused about how, exactly, an ideology of 'amicable ethnic separation' might differ from white nationalism."[14]

---

12 Horrell, *Ethnicity and Inclusion*, 313.

13 Horrell, *Ethnicity and Inclusion*, 318.

14 Kelefa Sanneh, "How Christian Is Christian Nationalism?" *New Yorker*, March 27, 2023, https://www.newyorker.com/magazine/2023/04/03/how-christian-is-christian-nationalism. See also Paul D. Miller, "A Tale of Two Books, One Podcast, and the Contest over Christian Nationalism," *Christianity Today,* December 20, 2022, https://www.christianitytoday.com/ct/2022/december-web-only/stephen-wolfe-case-christian-nationalism-paul-miller.html. Wolfe has since disaffiliated with Achord.

To susceptibility to white supremacy, we might add the susceptibility of Wolfe's case to autocracy. Wolfe disavows a yen for autocracy (279). However, his hope and awe for a great Christian prince who could be regarded as holding an office "most like God," being a veritable "image of Christ to his people," and "a national god" (286, 309, 289) certainly portray an extremely powerful individual. People conditioned to expect such a leader might easily be docile and vulnerable to autocratic, even dictatorial, actions on the part of that leader. Concomitantly, Wolfe wants the Christian prince and others to guard against "any injury to souls of the people of God," as well as prevent "the subversion of Christian government, Christian culture, or spiritual discipline" and "civil disruption or unrest" (359). These broad and vague worries are wide open to abuse and the tyranny of sensitive or over-scrupulous minorities (or majorities). What exactly counts as "subversion" of Christian government or culture? Is "civil disruption or unrest" registered as any protest, however peaceful or respectful? For determinations on all such matters, apparently we are simply supposed to trust the great prince—certainly an attitude that lends itself more to autocracy than democracy.

Another concern relates to a matter that would surely provoke much civil unrest. Namely, whose Christianity will define and enact Christian nationalism? Wolfe unabashedly wants conservative Reformed Protestants in charge. Others friendly to Christian nationalism include the Catholic integralists, who want government suffused with Christian principles but ultimately answering to Catholic doctrines and the Catholic magisterium.[15] They are on a collision course with Protestant nationalists, obviously. There are Southern Baptist nationalists who would surely accept the mantle of leadership and definition. To step outside this world of discourse, why not let Black Baptists, some of whom are friendly to Christian nationalism, head up the effort? The point is that determining whose Christian civil administration is best or most deserving is

---

15 For an excellent introduction to and critique of Catholic integralism, see Kevin Vallier, *All the Kingdoms of the World: On Radical Religious Alternatives to Liberalism* (New York: Oxford University Press, 2023).

no open-and-shut endeavor but one all too likely—once the door is opened—to lead to protracted, even violent conflict.[16]

Finally, I arrive at the most specifically theological of my concerns with Wolfe's Christian nationalism. However open one is or is not to natural law, in Wolfe's case it totally eclipses eschatology. Wolfe cannot allow for the eschatological gospel of the kingdom come in Christ to so much as add to, modify, or merely "critique" perceived natural law (50, 105, 24). Natural law, if it is not to remain uselessly vague and platitudinous, if it is actually to have teeth, must be precisely promulgated and interpreted. And such promulgators and interpreters are always human. Jesus's battles with his coreligionists (and the Roman authorities) were not couched in terms of natural law but surely all were struggling for what was thought to have been most "natural" in the sense of "right" and "truly fitting to being human." And in this context Jesus was seen as novel, disruptive, and civilly disturbing. In other words, he rocked many people's idea of what we might now refer to as natural law. The classic Christian confession is that Jesus Christ, in his life and death, presents to us the supreme picture of being truly and fully human. In this sense, he did indeed critique what people regarded as something like what we now call natural law.

Examples are numerous, but I focus here on one especially dear to Wolfe: family, and family's usefulness as an analogy for a Christian nation and its governance. For Wolfe, family is sacrosanct and preeminent. The family establishes and embodies as a microcosm what and how a Christian nation should be. (For some of many references to the family and its centrality, see 25, 139, 167, 180, 214, and 368.) If anything epitomizes natural law for Wolfe, it would be

---

16 Wolfe's answer to this dilemma is that America was founded by and most belongs to Anglo-Protestants. "As such, the whole tradition—between the early settlements to the early American republic—is an American, ethno-cultural inheritance that must be reclaimed and serve as an animating element of American Christian nationalism and a resource for American renewal" (431). But this answer only exacerbates significant concerns about Christian nationalism being for white Protestants, only or supremely.

the family. And yet consider how Jesus, as theologian Willie James Jennings says, "tore open ancient kinship networks."[17]

> Do not think that I have come to bring peace to the earth; I have not come to bring peace, but a sword. For I have come to set a man against his father, and a daughter against her mother, and a daughter-in-law against her mother-in-law; and one's foes will be members of one's own household. Whoever loves father or mother more than me is not worthy of me; and whoever loves son or daughter more than me is not worthy of me; and whoever does not take up the cross and follow me is not worthy of me. (Matt 10:34–38)

These words of Jesus, and the gospel in general, by no means destroy the family or familial affections. But they do decenter, relativize, and contextualize them in the kingdom of God. They open up kinship networks to the wide world and warn against marriages that focus exclusively on the couple and its hermetic world, not open to hospitality, turning "toward the narcissism of the two made one."[18] In this and so many other ways, Jesus eschatologically breaks into the old world, brings new wine and fresh wineskins (Matt 9:17; Mark 2:22; Luke 5:38), and introduces a new creation (2 Cor 5:17).

We may also note that a nation as family writ large fits clumsily at best with democracy. As Miller says, "One problem with this view is that families are dictatorships: children are subjects, not citizens. When we treat the nation as a large family, the president or head of state is a patriarch and we, his children: the template is not conducive to equality under the law or to democratic accountability."[19] No doubt Wolfe is ready to argue about the inadequacies of democracy.

---

17 Willie James Jennings, *Acts* (Louisville: Westminster John Knox, 2017), 54.

18 Jennings, *Acts,* 55. See my *Families at the Crossroads: Beyond Traditional and Modern Options* (Downers Grove, IL: InterVarsity, 2993) and, for a brief discussion, my *Naming Neoliberalism*, 92–97.

19 Miller, *Religion of American Greatness*, 74.

I do not have space to mount a defense for the Christian fitness of democracy but simply comment, with the great twentieth-century theologian Karl Barth, that democracy's shortcomings are not best resolved by its abolition.[20]

I do not intend to put Jesus and eschatology at loggerheads with natural law. I am suggesting that eschatology may bring us to new understandings of what is natural, and that we are first and last to look to Jesus as the supreme interpreter of truly natural law. For, again, one issue with natural law is that it is far from always self-apparent. The ancient Romans, for instance, considered it natural to expose unwanted infants to the elements. And Christians in the old American South considered racialized slavery entirely natural. What I object to in Wolfe is too much protology, too little eschatology.[21] For without close and ongoing attention to the eschatological Jesus of the Gospels, "Jesus" becomes an empty cipher to be filled with the content of our own predilections and "natural law" becomes but an excuse to baptize what we have already determined we want.[22]

DIAGNOSTIC QUESTIONS

Of course, Stephen Wolfe's is but one rendition of Christian national-ism. Others will be on offer, all proposing how Christians in America

---

20 See Eberhard Busch, *Karl Barth: His Life from Letters and Autobiographical Texts* (Eugene, OR: Wipf and Stock, 2976), 106.

21 Protology concerns the study of origins.

22 Rowan Williams posits three decisive critiques against theocracy: (1) It "assumes there can be an end to dialogue and discovery; that believers would have the right (if they had the power) to outlaw unbelief. It assumes a situation in which believers in effect had nothing to learn, and therefore that the corporate conversion of the church would be over and done with." (2) It assumes the end of history prematurely and presumptively, whereas history between the resurrection of Christ and his parousia is "the gift of a time of repentance and growth." (3) It "reflects a misunderstanding of the hope for God's kingdom, a fusion of divine and earthly sovereignty in a way quite foreign to the language and practice of Jesus." Rowan Williams, "Postmodern Theology and the Judgement of the World," in *Theology after Liberalism: A Reader,* ed. John Webster and George P. Schner (Oxford: Blackwell, 2000), 327.

can live not out of control, but back in control. In the meantime, I offer a brief set of diagnostic questions for clarification of what Christian nationalism may entail. These, and other questions like them, may help you to determine how friendly, really, you are to Christian nationalism.

- Should Congress declare America a Christian nation?
- Should Jews, Muslims, and other non-Christians be allowed as lawmakers?
- Do you want women to be subordinated in the home, church, and government?
- Do you, with Wolfe, wish for a great man, even a strong-man, who will reinstitute Christendom and Christian nationalism?
- What sort of Christianity should head up and lead an American Christian nation? Roman Catholicism? Prot-estantism—and, if so, what exact sort of Protestantism?
- Is "natural law" in any sense modified or critiqued by eschatology?
- How oppressed are Christian Americans today? Are they/we living under a kind of secular imperialism and captivity?
- How do you think that you and others of your race (or religion) will fare under Christian nationalism?[23]

---

23 It may seem obvious that non-Christians would not be "Christian" nationalists. But as sociologists Philip Gorski and Samuel Perry observe, the term "Christian" for some Christian nationalists "is far more akin to a dog whistle that calls an aggrieved tribe than a description of the content of one's faith." They report that more than 15 percent of those who in this context identify as "Christian" also say they are secular or belong to another religion. "What's more, nearly 19% of those who identify as 'evangelical' also identify as 'secular' or belong to a non-Christian religion. . . . Clearly, religious terms like 'Christian' and 'evangelical' are becoming markers of social identity and political views rather than just religious conviction." Philip Gorski and Samuel Perry, *The Flag and the Cross: White Christian Nationalism and the Threat to American Democracy* (New York: Oxford University Press, 2022), 44, 107.

- Are you prepared and willing to kill others—including other professing Christians—in order to institute Christian nationalism?

I am not so naive as to think such questions will dissuade deeply committed Christian nationalists, though I think those only vaguely and tenuously attracted to Christian nationalism may be dissuaded—or at least given pause. At any rate, the rest of us have been warned.

CHAPTER SIX

The Anarchistic Tendency
and Christian Citizenship

We resume our discussion of the church living out of control, but
now with a reversal of the direction of the preposition. Formerly,
living out *of* control has focused on the church not lording it over
others. Now we will focus on a proper sense in which the church and
Christians are to live out of the control of—that is, under—others.
In short, biblical Christianity invites us to embrace anarchism, or
at least an anarchistic tendency.

It will be helpful up front to make clear the sorts of anarchy I am
not calling Christians to embody. First, I am not arguing for anarchy
in the sophomoric sense of a purely destructive and cynical stance, as
in "tear it all down." Second, I am not, as with the anarchist movement originating in the nineteenth century, denying God's lordship
and sovereignty over humanity. Due in no small part to the historical
church's all-too-often and unfortunate embrace of the status quo
hierarchy, these anarchists sloganeered, "Neither God nor [human]
master." The anarchistic tendency I am interested in promoting is
emphatically not atheistic. Third, I am not arguing that the state is
always exploitative and unjust and should always be scorned and
resisted. As the anthropologist James Scott observes, "Americans
need only recall the scene of the federalized National Guard leading

black children to school through a menacing crowd of angry whites in Little Rock, Arkansas, in 1957 to realize that the state can, *in some circumstances*, play an emancipatory role."[1] Fourth, I am not arguing that the state alone tends to be dangerous and oppressive. For example, consider also neoliberalism, the enacted ideology that would have the market rule over all aspects of our lives.[2] A properly Christian anarchy will be aware of and sensitive to overweening powers and principalities of all sorts. Fifth, and finally, I do not expect that a true and beneficent anarchy can be realized on earth—at least not this side of the eschaton.[3]

Biblical glimmers of a kind of anarchism can be found in the prophets Isaiah and Ezekiel, who on occasion behaved unconventionally and outside common moralism. God instructs Isaiah to strip and walk about naked for three years, "as a sign and portent against Egypt and Ethiopia" (Isa 20:3). For his part, Ezekiel hears God tell him to lie on his side for more than a year, baking bread over a fire burning human dung. This is meant as a demonstration that an unrepentant Israel will be driven out among the nations, doomed to eat unclean bread. Unwilling to defile himself, Ezekiel is able to negotiate cow dung as a substitute fuel (Ezek 4:9–15).

Picking up on this and New Testament texts such as Paul's declaration that Christians are "fools for the sake of Christ" (1 Cor 4:10), later Christianity evolved the tradition of the holy fool. Especially popular in Russia, holy fools slept rough, were homeless, feigned insanity, and taunted people in power. With such challenges to

---

1 James C. Scott, *Two Cheers for Anarchism: Six Easy Pieces on Autonomy, Dignity, and Meaningful Work and Play* (Princeton, NJ: Princeton University Press, 2012), xiii–xiv.

2 See my *Naming Neoliberalism*.

3 Jacques Ellul draws this contrast in his usual forceful fashion: "The true anarchist thinks that an anarchist society—with no state, no organization, no hierarchy, and no authorities—is possible, livable, practicable. But I do not. In other words, I believe that the anarchist fight, the struggle for an anarchist society, is essential, but I also think that the realizing of such a society is impossible." Ellul, *Anarchy and Christianity*, 19.

conventional morality, status-seeking, and hierarchy, they were anarchists of a sort.

ORTHODOX ANARCHISTS AND OTHER SURPRISES

For consideration of Christian anarchy in our time and place, I know of few better guides than the innovative Orthodox theologian Davor Džalto. Rather than oxymoronically speaking of anarchy as a grand system or universalizing schema, Džalto writes of the anarchistic "tendency." Such a tendency focuses on "concrete cases of oppression and power structures in order to reduce the amount of oppression, change the (oppressive) power dynamics, and arrive at a more just and free social order."[4] Such a tendency means not deciding once and for all to be for or against culture (and its politics), but rather engaging culture on an ad hoc or case-by-case basis.[5] Especially given any culture's fluidity and variegated quality, the church may favor certain of its practices (music, medicine) while disfavoring others (patriarchalism, slavery). As Džalto puts it, "One should (re) act in a real (and ever changing) context, fighting what, in each given historical period and in each given society, is the greatest threat to human freedom and dignity."[6]

Signally, Džalto's Christian anarchy is grounded in eschatology. "[F]rom an Orthodox Christian perspective, no social or political order (or lack thereof) will ever be able to represent an 'ideal' form of interhuman relations, since, from the Christian point of view, the only 'ideal' form of human existence is the Kingdom of God as an eschatological reality. This (fully manifested) Kingdom cannot be established within the boundaries of the world we are in and in the

---

4 Davor Džalto, *Anarchy and the Kingdom of God: From Eschatology to Orthodox Political Theology and Back* (New York: Fordham University Press, 2021), 15.

5 For an extended discussion of ad hoc politics, see my *Naming Neoliberalism*, 132–134.

6 Džalto, *Anarchy and the Kingdom of God*, 20.

historical process as we know it. In history, we can only have a glimpse of it, as 'in a mirror, darkly.'"[7] In other words, so long as history lasts, Christians will be perpetually dissatisfied. Awaiting the eschaton, the church is ever on a pilgrimage, never fully at home. It will not confuse any political or cultural arrangement with the kingdom of God arrived in its completeness or perfection. It remains vigilant against oppression of all sorts and in fact "remains skeptical toward the social-political sphere as such, as this sphere is the result of our existence in history and in 'this world,' the existence that needs to be transfigured to conform to the logic of free eschatological existence."[8]

So, in a way and to a degree, Christians "sit loose" to the world's politics and governments. Their eye remains always "on the prize," so to speak, the prize of God's kingdom come and coming. A "Christian 'anarchist,' looking upon the social-political from a theological perspective, is primarily interested in the new mode of existence, and the communion with God and the rest of creatures in the eschatological reality of the Kingdom of God. Social and political structures as such do not have, in this perspective, any real meaning or significance per se. They are a 'necessary evil,' which may be changed but can never be turned into something immanently *good* or *just*, something that would satisfy Christian eschatological maximalism."[9] Consequently, "Christians should never mistake the goals, concerns, and structures that belong to 'this world' with the real goal of Christian life—new creation and communion with God and the entirety of creation."[10]

Džalto's "eschatological maximalism" entails that the politics of this world, however radical, are never radical enough. They do not cut to the root of the world's captivity and illness. They remain mired in penultimate struggles that they absolutize as ultimate and are constantly

---

7 Džalto, *Anarchy and the Kingdom of God*, 1.

8 Džalto, *Anarchy and the Kingdom of God*, 15.

9 Džalto, *Anarchy and the Kingdom of God*, 12.

10 Džalto, *Anarchy and the Kingdom of God*, 13. An important biblical text in this vein is 1 Corinthians 7:29–31, where Paul counsels Christians to graciously inhabit the forms of this age (marriage, temporal mourning and rejoicing, wealth), but "as though" or "as if" they were not, "For the present form of this world is passing away."

prone to settle on one political order or another as the best humanity can hope for, and then to dehumanize or demonize those who think a different political order is that best hope. Accordingly, the problem "with most political theologies (Orthodox or not) is that they almost instinctively defend the dominant systems of power in which they operate, be it 'conservative' or 'liberal,' 'democratic' or autocratic. Theology there effectively functions as a political ideology giving metaphysical significance to political institutions."[11] When theology and politics so operate, "the very need for the eschaton, for the future kingdom of God, is obscured. The empire (state) replaces the eschatological Kingdom." Then, and just so, the state becomes "an idol."[12]

A similar understanding and attitude comes through not only in Džalto, but in another Christian thinker with anarchistic tendencies, the late Church of the Brethren theologian Vernard Eller. He notices that worldly politics "rests upon a quite unfounded confidence in the moral competency of human beings—and more particularly, upon a quite arrogant error in attributing categorical moral superiority to partisans of the one 'true' ideology over against those of any party else."[13] Because it is not truly radical, "a prime characteristic of worldly politics is its invariable forming of itself as 'adversarial contest,'"[14] a contest in which each side comes to imagine itself as the only and supremely true and just force. And as such the politics formed on this basis becomes impositional, set on imposing its will on the "other side."

It is exactly here that the radicality of Jesus's politics shows itself. As Eller writes, "When Jesus said 'My kingdom is not of this world,' he was saying that although all worldly [powers] *have* to be impositional, his is radically different in that it does not have to be—and in fact is not."[15] Jesus chose to live out of control and called his church also to live nonimpositionally, out of control. Particularly, "as God

---

11 Džalto, *Anarchy and the Kingdom of God,* 112.

12 Džalto, *Anarchy and the Kingdom of God,* 114.

13 Vernard Eller, *Christian Anarchy: Jesus' Primacy over the Powers* (Eugene, OR: Wipf and Stock, 1987), xii.

14 Eller, *Chrisitan Anarchy,* xii.

15 Eller, *Christian Anarchy,* 3.

has been revealed in Jesus Christ, the style of his [power] is not that of imposition but of the opposite, namely, that of the cross, the self-givingness of agape-love. And . . . God's [power], his will for us, is never anything extraneous to ourselves but precisely that which is most germane to our true destiny and being."[16] Džalto also points to Jesus's radicality in this regard:

Christ's Kingdom does not pose a threat to the political system and political power in the same way in which other kingdoms (and other types of power and authority) do. Christ is not another political leader, a protagonist of another political movement or ideology who or which would fight to rule over people. Instead, he poses a threat to the power and authority at a much more fundamental level—by questioning the very logic upon which the political authority, rule, and domination is built, and by refusing to submit to that logic and give it a metaphysical legitimacy. The Kingdom of God is not of "this world"—it cannot be realized within the boundaries and logic of "this world." It overcomes "this world" by offering a different logic of being.[17]

Thus does Jesus include among his disciples radically opposed partisans: both zealots who would kill to vanquish Rome and tax collectors who are seen as abject collaborators with Rome. Thus does Jesus ever and always choose to follow the will of his Father, who makes rain and sunshine fall on all persons, of whatever parties. Thus does Jesus confound his "opponents" at every turn, as they struggle to label (and so dismiss) him once and for all. Thus does Jesus refuse violence even to the extent of death on a shameful cross, embracing and forgiving all, including his tormentors. And finally, thus does Jesus rise from the dead, vindicated as the Messiah, the true savior from sin and death.

---

16 Eller, *Christian Anarchy*, 6.

17 Džalto, *Anarchy and the Kingdom of God*, 193.

Living out of control with anarchistic tendencies requires nimbleness and constant shrewdness. It means never settling on a single worldview, ideology, political party, or, indeed, a single national commitment. It entails vigilance to "always be on the side of those oppressed and suffering, and always skeptical and critical of the ideological mainstream, never accepting any narratives that are used against concrete human beings, even when these claim to be the most noble, ethical, and progressive." At the same time, it means remembering that oppressors, too, are created in the image of God and invited to repentance and salvation. "We can condemn their actions, but never reject concrete human beings."[18] So living out of control above all means trusting that God has acted definitively in the life, death, and resurrection of Jesus—this faith, this trust, held alone ultimately and finally. Accordingly, living out of control means living by the surprises that the kingdom always brings our way. "Without an eschatological awareness in our interaction with the everyday, we cannot but become immune to surprise and, therefore, to the kingdom of God, which has surprise as its very mode of manifestation (Matt 24:27; Mark 13:36; Luke 12:40; 17:24)."[19]

For a modern exemplar and master of Christian anarchistic tendencies, consider Karl Barth. Living through the tumultuous mid-twentieth century, amid World War II and then the Cold War, the Swiss Reformed theologian was heavily and constantly politically engaged. Yet he could declare that we should do theology as if nothing had happened. "Above all," he said, "it will be a matter of recognizing God once more as God. . . . This is a task alongside

---

18 Džalto, *Anarchy and the Kingdom of God,* 215 and 216. The dialectical skill of both siding with the oppressed and reaching out to oppressors was strikingly demonstrated by the Southern preacher Will Campbell, who stood clearly and constantly against racism while also ministering to bigots. See especially his *Brother to a Dragonfly* (Jackson, MS: University of Mississippi Press, 1977).

19 John Panteleimon Mannoussakis, "The Anarchic Principle of Christian Eschatology in the Eucharistic Tradition of the Eastern Church," *Harvard Theological Review* 100, no. 1 (2007): 33, https://www.jstor.org/stable/4125233.

which all cultural, social, and patriotic duties are child's play."[20] And, people "can never make 'God's standpoint their own partisan standpoint' and therefore no individual or group simply stands on God's side over against others. . . . All human distinctions—between the religious and irreligious, the moral and the immoral—become relative. . . . [For] the kingdom of God is not 'a rebellion within the old aeon but the dawn of a new one'; it is not 'a development of previous possibilities but the new possibility of life.'"[21] So while Barth stood boldly and controversially against the Nazification of German Christians, and even served in the Swiss army, once the war was done he switched sympathies to the defeated Germans. While calling them to confession of their monumental guilt, he petitioned the Allied powers against crushing and ill treatment of the defeated. Karl Barth's lifelong witness, which seemingly came out of nowhere, was another one of God's surprises.[22]

THE ANARCHIST TENDENCY AND
DISPUTED BIBLICAL TEXTS

If there is a theme text for the Christian anarchistic tendency, it could be Colossians 2:15: "[Through the cross, Jesus] disarmed the rulers and authorities and made a public example of them, triumphing over them in it." The passion/suffering of Christ at the crucifixion revealed the true character of the powers at their worst: demonic, violent, and out of control. In being made a "public example" (or "spectacle," as in other translations) the powers unwittingly were unmasked by an encounter with God as very God. The religious and

---

20 Busch, *Karl Barth*, 89.

21 Busch, *Karl Barth,* 100. This is Busch's framing; interior quotes come directly from Barth.

22 For a further sense of Barth's brilliant theopolitical witness, see Timothy J. Gorringe, *Karl Barth: Against Hegemony* (New York: Oxford University Press, 1999), and Christiane Tietz, *Karl Barth: A Life in Conflict* (Oxford: Oxford University Press, 2021).

political authorities were shown, in their desperate lethality, not to be purely benign and benevolent. The cross unmasked their darker nature and intentions and showed them not to be the saviors and winsome gods they pretend to be in their absolutization. Once and for all, their true colors were uncovered and flown. Ever after, following in the way of Jesus, the church knows and reveals to all that accepting and surrendering to death out of love and forgiveness disarms the powers—legal, political, cultural, religious, and so forth—and it does so without "increasing the sum of evil in the world."[23]

By way of (only apparent) contrast, there are two other texts that are often used to argue against Christian anarchistic tendencies. Mark 12:13–17 and Romans 13:1–7 have been employed all too frequently (one might almost say classically) to push Christians and others into line, to make them passive and pliable to the ruling powers of any period.

Mark 12:13–17 (and its parallels at Matthew 22:23–33 and Luke 20:27–38) operates with a controversial question of the time as its background. Jews were divided on submitting to the Romans by paying taxes or resisting them by withholding taxes. The authorities, enamored of their own cleverness, think they can cripple Jesus's moral authority by forcing him to choose a side in this hotly contested debate. However he chooses, he will enrage one faction or the other—thus both losing followers and bringing one or another set of authorities down on his head. Consider the Markan text in full:

Then they sent to him some Pharisees and some Herodians to trap him in what he said. And they came and said to him, "Teacher, we know that you are sincere, and show deference to no one; for you do not regard people with partiality, but teach the way of God in accordance with truth. Is it lawful to pay taxes to the emperor, or not? Should we pay them, or should we not?" But knowing their hypocrisy, he said to them,

---

23 Ellul, as quoted in Alexandre Christoyannopoulos, *Christian Anarchy: A Political Commentary on the Gospel* (Exeter: Imprint Academic, 2011), 99. See Christoyannopoulos's entire discussion of Colossians 2:15 at 95–99.

"Why are you putting me to the test? Bring me a denarius and let me see it." And they brought one. Then he said to them, "Whose head is this, and whose title?" They answered, "The emperor's." Jesus said to them, "Give to the emperor the things that are the emperor's, and to God the things that are God's." And they were utterly amazed at him.

Read anti-anarchistically, this text is purported to show that Jesus reserves to his followers only the ethereal, private realm of the spiritual (the nonmaterial) and the emotional (the interior or psychological) and grants material and the physical, outward reality to the disposal of Caesar. Such a reading immediately and profoundly runs afoul of the robust Jewish insistence, to the contrary, that everything—material as well as spiritual, physical as well as emotional—belongs to the God of Israel, the sole creator of the world in every one of its aspects.

"[H]eaven and the heaven of heavens belong to the LORD, your God, the earth with *all* that is in it . . ." (Deut 10:14)

"For *all* things come from you, and of your own have we given you." (1 Chr 29:14)

"The earth is the LORD's and *all* that is in it . . ." (Ps 24:1)

"The heavens are yours, the earth also is yours; the world and *all* that is in it—you have founded them." (Ps 89:11)

Jesus can in no way be credibly seen as here denying this key and sweeping Jewish conviction. What he does instead is ask his challengers to produce a denarius, a coin of about a day's wage, minted by the Romans. The coin bears the image of Caesar, the emperor. When Jesus has his challengers confirm as much, he declares, "Give to the emperor the things that are the emperor's, and to God the things that are God's." What Jesus means to do is not to divvy up reality, some belonging to Caesar and some to God, but simply to declare that Caesar, having created money, is money's master. That and nothing more. And we should not forget what stark, severe, and delimiting words Jesus has for the sway of Mammon. Everything belongs to God, as the Jewish tradition and texts roundly affirm, "and Caesar is legitimate master of nothing but what he fabricates for himself."[24] What a puny realm that is in comparison to God's domain! Thus "Render unto Caesar" (to use the King James wording), far from being a text that quashes all Christian anarchistic tendencies, in fact confirms them. "And they were utterly amazed at him"—for, standing apart from and above both the taxpaying collaborators and the resistant tax withholders, he foxily and confoundingly called his followers to live out from under the control and definitions of the powers and principalities.

What of Romans 13:1–7, which famously instructs Christians to "be subject to the governing authorities," who do not "bear the sword [i.e., coercive force] in vain" but as "a servant of God"? Most importantly, it is crucial to read this passage in context, and two contexts at that.

The first context is the Apostle Paul's full life and witness. The same Paul who wrote the Letter to the Romans frequently acted against the edicts and will of the governing authorities. Thus, he suffered imprisonments and "countless floggings" (2 Cor 11:23). Three times, he tells us, "I was beaten with rods" (2 Cor 11:25), a specifically Roman punishment.[25] Furthermore, he would have known that, "only a few years earlier, the Christians of Rome (to whom he was writing), under the edict of Claudius, had their congregations broken up and dispersed."[26] So the governmental authorities disrupted the ministries of Paul and the Roman church, and severely abused Paul's person (even eventually executing him). Consequently, to read

---

24 Jacques Ellul, "Anarchism and Christianity," *Katallagete* 7, no. 3 (Fall 1980): htpps://theanarchistlibrary.org/library/jacques-ellul-anarchism-and-christianity-en.html.

25 Thompson, *Christ and Culture in the New Testament*, 87.

26 Eller, *Christian Anarchy*, 198.

Romans 13 as a blanket approval of any and every governmental sanction "should be held off as our last possible alternative of interpretation rather than welcomed as the first."[27]

The second crucial context is the situation of Romans 13:1–7 in the entire text of the letter to the Romans, and particularly following chapter 12. Chapter 12 ends with the counsel for Christians to love their enemies. "Bless those who persecute you; bless and do not curse them. . . . No, 'if your enemies are hungry, feed them; if they are thirsty, give them something to drink; for by doing this you will heap burning coals on their heads.' Do not be overcome by evil, but overcome evil with good" (Rom 12:14, 20–21). From there Paul moves directly and immediately to "Let every person be subject to the governing authorities" (Rom 13:1). Surely Eller is correct to argue, "The 'governing authorities,' then, are brought in as Paul's example of those to whom it will be most difficult to make the obligation [to love even enemies] apply—but whom God nevertheless commands us to love, even when our natural propensity most strongly urges us to hate, resist, and fight them." In its immediate context, "Paul is using the governing authorities as a test case of our loving the enemy."[28]

In addition, notice that Paul designates the governing authority as God's "servant" (Rom 13:4–5). Thus Paul subordinates Caesar, against Caesar's own will and intention, to the God of Israel met in Jesus Christ. Putting Romans 13:1–7 in context, and noting Caesar's demotion from lordship of all he surveys, we can see that this text is not a carte blanche for all of government and its actions. Rather, it allows that God is able to co-opt governmental authorities to God's purposes in *some* ways and in *some* instances. As Douglas Harink says, "Human societies and nations continue to belong to God and to be held in being by God, because God in his sovereignty and freedom is able to, and does, work through *some* of the workings of political authorities for God's own purposes."[29] And as

---

27 Eller, *Christian Anarchy*, 199.

28 Eller, *Christian Anarchy*, 197.

29 Harink, *Resurrecting Justice*, 183.

Jacques Ellul concludes, "Political authority and organizations are necessities of *social life* but *nothing more than necessities.* They are constantly tempted to take the place of God, for the magistrate or king infallibly regards themselves as authority *per se.* This power must be contested, denied and constantly challenged. It becomes acceptable only when it stays within its humble status, when it is weak, when it serves the good (which is extremely rare) and truly transforms itself into the servant of humanity (since it is already the servant of God!)."[30] Accordingly, the Christian anarchistic tendency is not denied or eliminated in Romans 13. Any extreme tendencies it may have are tempered; Christians are warned not to revolt and commanded to pay taxes. But ultimately they make (much) less of the principalities and powers than the powers make of themselves, they constantly challenge the powers' overreach, and they root all their behavior in a Christocentric love that often can only baffle worldly authorities.

A final comment: governmental authorities play an important role when the church fails so grossly as to itself become and operate like the principalities and powers. At times the institutionalized church has sinned, has acted illegally, and to protect its institutional prerogatives (property, wealth) has not corrected itself. The most flagrant recent example is surely the heinous sexual abuse—across the traditions, in Roman Catholic and Protestant purviews—that was finally uncovered and prosecuted despite the resistance and grudging admissions of church authorities. In such cases, God works through one principality and power to correct another principality and power. Surely then the government has not borne the sword in vain.

ON CHRISTIAN CITIZENSHIP

A Christian, eschatologically determined anarchy then is the basis of the church's relationship to governmental politics. At its best,

---

30 Ellul, "Anarchism and Christianity."

Christian engagement in governmental politics always makes clear where its ultimate and final allegiance lies—with Christ and the kingdom of God, and not with any given nation or political party. Yet this does not rule out Christian engagement in governmental politics, or Christian citizenship in the world.

Significantly, all cats are not indistinguishably gray in the darkness or semi-twilight of worldly politics. The church hopes and works for the most proximately just and true government in any given situation. It can, for instance, favor fallibly democratic polities over fascist polities. Christians with anarchistic tendencies may judge one human power or government as better, relatively speaking, than another, and be grateful for that. Eller cites the example of his Brethren forebears who fled persecuting German powers for the comparatively free government of William Penn, in the early United States. They knew they were trading a "bad [power] for a better one. And they were appropriately grateful to God for the change. But that from which their anarchy did preserve them was the confusing of Penn's [governmental power] with the kingdom of God."[31] The church can and should come alongside those struggling for the immediate human good. At the same time, its eschatological perspective should prevent the church from crusades and from the practical deification of any worldly political force. In this manner, says Jacques Ellul, "Christians can be . . . more realistic and less ideological than others."[32]

When it comes to discernment about particular polities and governmental policies, Christians need to be aware that they are necessarily and unavoidably employing prudential reasoning. The gospel does not starkly dictate solutions to many (or most) of our worldly political quandaries. So prudence is required to reason

---

31 Eller, *Christian Anarchy*, 13. Taken to heart, a Christian anarchistic attitude and practice would go a long way toward defusing the extreme polarization America now suffers.

32 Ellul, *In Season, Out of Season*, 91.

from the wider and encompassing gospel mandate to measures to be recommended in particular circumstances. And prudence ineluctably involves interpretation and selectivity. For different reasoners, the pertinence of particular principles will differ, and emphasis will fall in different places. Consequently, Christians will disagree on particular political policies and actions. They may agree, for instance, that policies should alleviate or eliminate poverty but honestly differ on which policies will effectively do so. Debate and argument are unavoidable. At its best, the church will include all sorts of disciples who disagree on policies, and use open, truthful, and respectful debate to move forward. This side of the eschaton, any given church is at its strongest when its numbers contain (political) liberals and conservatives, capitalists and socialists, Democrats and Republicans.

Again, prudential reasoning is necessary and unavoidable in the rough and tumble of this-worldly, governmental politics. What we must not do is identify yours or my prudential reasoning with the gospel itself, or any given political party with the kingdom of God. Prudential reasoning means that we have *derived* our determination of a certain policy from the gospel. The derivation is not to be confused with the source, the flower with the root, the acorn with the oak. Procedural secularity, as discussed in chapter 4, allows for religious conviction to play a role in governmental politics. But policy and gospel are rarely simply identical. This means that when we enter the arena of governmental politics, though we may be motivated and roughly guided by the gospel, we can rarely argue only or thoroughly in theological terms, and we should never try to play an explicitly Christian trump card. This too is a feature of living out of control. And it requires the ongoing, constant translation of Christian language into other, secondary languages.

Perhaps nothing in American history better exemplifies this sort of political action than the Black church. As the Black Baptist minister and public intellectual Michael Eric Dyson points out, Martin Luther King Jr. and his cohorts "translated their religious efforts into the language with the best chance to express their goals in the national arena. For the black church, justice is what love sounds like when it speaks in public, civic piety is love's public language, equality its tone of voice, and freedom its constant pitch."[33] Dyson explains:

> Such acts of translation also rest on the black Christian belief that the entire world belongs to God, that religious truth is not bound to the sanctuary, and that God often employs apparently disinterested or even hostile persons, forces, and institutions to achieve the divine prerogative. This truth can be partially glimpsed in the popularity of the scripture "You meant evil against me; but God meant it for good." This often quoted passage forms one of the most visible hermeneutic strategies employed in the black church, one that reflects a strong doctrine of providence and a serviceable theodicy geared toward black survival and a momentous confrontation with suffering and evil.[34]

It is crucial to remember that theologically explicit language is our first and primary language as Christians, but Dyson is right to insist that "translation" is possible and important. As he says, "God is the original and ultimate polyglot."[35] The Black church reminds us all that governmental political engagement is a part of the Christian repertoire, while also demonstrating prefigurative and other Christian politics. It was in the church, across centuries of "the murder and maiming of black life," that Black Christians recognized and celebrated their rightful dignity, where janitors and maids claimed their royal patrimony (1 Pet 2:9), making them of no less value than white CEOs, generals, and presidents.[36] Black Christians called and call all

---

33 Michael Eric Dyson, "'God Almighty Has Spoken from Washington, D.C.': American Society and Christian Faith," in *The Michael Eric Dyson Reader* (New York: Basic Civitas, 2004), 187.

34 Dyson, "God Almighty Has Spoken from Washington, D.C.," 187–188.

35 Dyson, "God Almighty Has Spoken from Washington, D.C.," 188.

36 Dyson, "God Almighty Has Spoken from Washington, D.C.," 189.

would-be Christians to their best selves and highest convictions. King and his ministerial friends embodied and enacted the effectiveness of nonviolent change. And, not least, the Black church displays the power of faith, even when it is in the minority and out of control.

Let us, then, embrace the Christian anarchistic tendency *and* recognize that Christians are citizens in the world. We can live out of control in the sense of not lording it over others, and in the sense of coming out from under the control of others. The Black church shows that it can be so.

CHAPTER SEVEN

The Political Centrality of the Gospel
Proclamation and Eucharist

It is true that we Christians gather for worship only a few hours every week. Thus do some trivialize the potential and power of worship. But the lovemaking of a couple lasts only an hour or two every week, yet it immeasurably enriches their bond. Similarly, boot camp lasts a few months, but molds ordinary men and women into soldiers. To consider negative and ugly examples, the trauma of a robbery or a rape may last "mere" minutes, but it marks its victims for a lifetime.

It is a mistake, then, to think that the formative power of events and practices depend solely on their (long) duration. Other factors come into play. Their intentionality makes a difference. So does their intensity. Their authenticity also matters—the genuine love of our lovemaking couple sets their act apart in its formative effect from a fickle tryst between strangers.

I do not mean to overstate the power of communal worship. It is not magical. It does not automatically or necessarily produce saints. Nor should it stand in isolation, removed from daily acts of kindness, witness, and discipleship. But I think the potential of gathered worship is considerable and has been vitiated by our sometime tendencies to engage in it mindlessly and unimaginatively, and to privatize it—to consider it first and foremost as a transaction between the individual me and God. Instead, we should consider it our primary and most important *political* act. As Karl Barth has written,

> The freedom of Christians to call upon God as their Father, their living spiritual life in this freedom, and their life as a whole in its activation and development, is, of course, a very personal matter; but it is not a private matter. It is not a matter of the private salvation and bliss of the individual Christian, for the individual Christian can call upon God only as *our* Father. He can do so only as one among many brethren. Similarly, the brotherly fellowship of Christians, the Christian community, is not an organization for the common cultivation of the very private concerns of its individual members. *Their invocation of God is as such a supremely social matter, publicly social, not to say political and even cosmic.*[1]

After all, in communal worship the *ekklesia*, the Congress of God, gathers to declare and celebrate nothing less than that the Creator-Redeemer God has rescued all creation from its captivity to sin and death. The God of Israel met in Jesus Christ has "wonderfully created, and yet more wonderfully restored, the dignity of human nature."[2] God has ended humanity's enmity with God and with one another. God has acted and will act to heal the "whole creation" and release it from its bondage to decay (Rom 8:18–30). As Barth says, what could be more political, even more cosmic, than this? To put it in stately Latin, our worship is the declaration *Regum habemus*: "We have a king!"[3] And this king—not any Caesar, not any strongman, not any other power—is Lord and Savior of all.

Accordingly, there is something implicitly politically confrontational about gathered worship. It is a declaration, a repeated and embodied declaration, that we live out of our own control and out

---

1 Karl Barth, *Church Dogmatics* IV/4 (London: T & T Clark International), 95; latter emphasis added.

2 Book of Common Prayer, Collect "Of the Incarnation," 252.

3 Ernst Käsemann, *Church Conflicts: The Cross, Apocalyptic, and Political Resistance* (Grand Rapids: Baker Academic, 2021), 65.

from under the control of any power other than God. In Israel and Jesus Christ, God has acted nothing less than apocalyptically, ending one age and inaugurating another, revealing who is truly in control of the world and of history. As such, apocalyptic "offers a way of imaging what happens when this radically different mode of life [in and under Christ the King] confronts or is confronted by the powers and principalities that currently rule human imaginations and arrangements."[4]

Entered into with awareness, openness, attention, and intention, communal worship is necessarily and unfailingly intense, engaging in the highest imaginable stakes. Of course we are often bored in our pews, our minds adrift. But again, is not the lover sometimes bored with her lover, the soldier at boot camp's mind frequently adrift on other matters? When we keep at it, with intentionality and attention, the liturgy, through the Spirit, will change us. And it can endlessly fascinate and captivate us. For it is "a carousel of sayings and stories, songs and prayers, processions and silences, images and visions, symbols and rituals, feasts and fasts in which the mysterious ways of God are not merely presented but experienced, not merely perused but lived through."[5]

With all this said, I want to dwell on the two major aspects of liturgy, of communal worship: the word (or proclamation) and the sacrament (Eucharist—or, as it is called in traditions other than my own, the Lord's Supper, Mass, or simply Communion). The focus will rest on how proclamation and Eucharist rehearse the gospel, and on the gospel's unsurpassed political significance.

POLITICAL GOOD TIDINGS FOR ALL

You will recall that the *evangel,* the gospel or good news, was understood in its original cultural context as an explicitly political action. It was the announcement that an heir had been born to Caesar, that

---

4 Winn, *Jesus, Jubilee, and the Politics of God's Reign,* 9.

5 Mark Searle, quoted in Nicholas Denysenko, *This Is the Day that the Lord Has Made: The Liturgical Year in Orthodoxy* (Eugene, OR: Cascade, 2023), 3.

a decisive battle had been won, that slaves had been freed, that a new king had ascended to the throne, or the like. Adapted by Christians, the gospel was transposed to a theological key but without losing one iota of its political denotation and connotation. The gospel was and is the proclamation that the heir of Israel's promises was born in a manger, that the captor's sin and death had been defeated, that an enslaved humanity had been liberated, and that a new King now reigns above all others. "This," says Barth, "is what the New Testament means by 'preaching.' The event proclaimed is the coming of the kingdom, the fulfilment of the lordship of God on earth, its concrete institution in direct contrast to all human lordships and kingdoms, the striking of the last hour for these dominions however long they may still persist, the once for all, complete and irrevocable seizure of power by God as a historical reality among men."[6]

The sermon is meant to proclaim this startlingly good news, and to make it come alive and relevant in the particular historical situation of the listening, praying congregation. This preaching uniquely does. As the ecumenical and liturgical theologian Geoffrey Wainwright puts it, "The continued reading of the scriptures in church keeps the vocabulary, grammar and syntax of the biblical revelation before the people. With the aid of the preacher as interpreter of scripture, the people's ears become attuned to hear the voice of God speak to them in their present circumstances."[7] But the general proclamation of the gospel occurs in all aspects of the liturgy. The Eucharist is saturated with biblical texts and declares the gospel roundly and explicitly. For instance, the celebrant and the people together "proclaim the mystery of faith":

Christ has died.

Christ is risen.

Christ will come again.[8]

---

6 Karl Barth, *Church Dogmatics* IV/2 (Edinburgh: T. & T. Clark, 2958), 204.

7 Geoffrey Wainwright, *Doxology: The Praise of God in Worship* (New York: Oxford University Press, 1980), 19.

8 Book of Common Prayer, Eucharistic Prayer A, 363.

Truly, then, word and sacrament, preaching and the Eucharist, are marks of the church in service to the gospel. But the German apocalyptic theologian Ernst Käsemann boldly insists on a third mark of the church. "[A]longside right doctrine and administration of the sacraments, a third criterion [defining the church] is indispensable— that is, the visible presence of the poor in the congregation and in worship. For liberation from earthly tyrants is part of the good news of the gospel."[9] He later elaborates,

> We are accustomed to defining the church on the basis of Word and Sacrament. Perhaps, on the basis of the gospel, we should add a third mark, in order to fend off spiritualism and on earth achieve a sharper profile. The Beatitudes at the beginning of the New Testament, and the Apocalypse of John at the end, do not allow us the least doubt that the Father of Jesus is a God who resists the proud, bestows grace on the lowly, draws near to the outcasts, the poor, and the suffering. The entire history of Israel points in the same direction. . . . No community deserves to be named after the Crucified that does not turn to the least, the helpless, the abandoned, the violated, to those who are not strong, wise, or pious in themselves, and thus make clear that the justification of the godless is projected right into the social dimension.[10]

The church's intent is not, by any means, to glorify poverty. Nor is it to imagine that the poor are innately sinless. Rather, the poor are those in our number who, surviving paycheck to paycheck, buffeted by social and political forces clearly larger and more powerful than them, always bearing the main brunt of any war, most readily admit that they live out of control, that they cannot save themselves. Those

---

9 Käsemann, *Church Conflicts*, 24.

10 Käsemann, *Church Conflicts*, 62–63. And: "I am no longer content with the [Lutheran] Augsburg Confession, since the visible Christian community is made known just as much in the presence of the poor . . . as in the preaching of the gospel and the administration of the sacraments" (225).

of us comparatively wealthy are not so much buffeted as buffered—we are buffered (and blinded) by our inheritances, our savings and stock portfolios, our insurance policies. So buffered, and often catered to by the political class, we more readily fantasize that we are in control of our lives and destinies, that we cannot only save ourselves but that we have already saved ourselves. This is why the gospel comes as unmitigated good news to the poor, but initially presents as a challenge to the rich, who are not so ready to admit that humanity cannot and has not saved itself. But what the poor readily admit is true in actuality for the rich as well. The gospel liberates us all and opens onto a greater, wonderfully more expansive reality for the entire creation. It truly is good news, for the poor and the rich. "Only in seeing again do I know that I was blind; that I was squatting in a prison becomes apparent only when the prison doors are open."[11]

TWO BIBLICAL MOTIFS OF THE ATONEMENT

Though the atonement, our salvation, is ultimately a gracious mystery, the New Testament exhibits two motifs about it in some abundance. The first motif is our reconciliation—with God, with one another, with all of creation.

Regarding reconciliation, it is first of all essential to recognize that God is not and has never been at enmity with humanity. The God of Israel is a loving creator, sustainer, and redeemer. From first to last, God is for humanity, on humanity's side. But the same cannot be said for humanity's attitude and comportment toward God. Humans are, innately and left to our own devices, enemies of God. Rather than living out of control and in God's loving guidance, we want to set our terms, decide good and evil for ourselves, determine our own destinies. This behavior, this habit, this "instinct" is self-destructive and against God's will for our true flourishing. Given humanity's self-destructive bent, it needs to be reconciled to God.

---

11 Dorothee Soelle, *The Silent Cry: Mysticism and Resistance* (Minneapolis: Fortress, 2001), 29.

In Christ, God overcomes our naturalized enmity from the inside out. Christ is the second Adam, the Adam who this time chooses not to be estranged from God but to remain in fellowship with God (Paul). In Christ, God is the Judge who is judged, assuming and overcoming the liabilities of human self-destruction.[12] Thus we are reconciled to God, to one another, and to all of creation.

The second motif of atonement is *Christus Victor*, or Christ the Victor. Like the theme of reconciliation, it is abundant in Pauline texts. *Christus Victor* declares that the two real enemies of human and creational welfare are sin and death, and that Christ in his crucifixion and resurrection has triumphed over these supreme enemies. Sin and death, along with the principalities and powers they employ, have rebelled against God and God's will for the beloved creation. Humanity, and the rest of creation, cannot save itself from or defeat these great and dark powers on its own. So, God in Christ has confronted and overcome them on our behalf. Christian Collins Winn puts it this way: "Human beings are enslaved by death-dealing powers that have revolted against God, with the result being the despoliation of creation and the physical and eschatological death of humanity, or its total separation from God. What is more, human beings are fundamentally incapable of standing against these powers."[13] With humanity and all of creation paralyzed and supine under the powers, God in Christ triumphantly invaded territory that God really owned but that had come under enemy occupation. *Christus Victor*—Christ is Victor!—is the great cry of gospel freedom.

POLITICAL POINTS FOR GOSPEL CENTERING

With those atonement motifs surveyed, it may be helpful to summarize the robust gospel points on which all Christian politics center.

---

12 See Barth's magisterial treatment of the Judge judged theme in *Church Dogmatics* IV/1 (Edinburgh: T. & T. Clark, 1956), 211–283.

13 Winn, *Jesus, Jubilee, and the Politics of God's Reign*, 74.

These are points or themes preachers should constantly proclaim, with awareness of their political ramifications.

- Salvation involves the entire cosmos, in all its aspects. God in Israel and Jesus Christ acts for all of humanity and its genuine flourishing. The gospel is not individualistic or a purely private matter. It is about the saving and healing of all creation, including the rocks and the trees, the dogs and the bees. This salvation potently includes our social and political characteristics that are innate and ineradicable to being human.
- Humanity cannot save itself. By habit and deep desire, it wants to; it is averse to the need for a savior outside itself. But the refusal to live out of control is ultimately an exercise in futility. So, as Barth says on the primacy of preaching the word of God, "By proclaiming the divine justification, [the church] performs the best service to the establishment and maintenance of human justice."[14] Preaching is an innately and supremely political act, pointing to true justice.
- Israel is the unique and irreplaceable elect people and Jesus is the elect among the elected who crowns the sustaining work of God on behalf of creation. Israel (and the church) is a royal people, a political body, and Jesus is the King of kings, a political actor.
- The church, following Israel, is God's central social and political body called to declare and embody in its worship and life the gospel and the kingdom it proclaims. So the Christian's ultimate politics is founded and enacted and declared supremely in the church.
- At the same time, the kingdom of God is bigger than the church. Accordingly, the church will look for signs of God's saving activity outside and not just inside its walls.

---

14 Busch, *Karl Barth*, 288.

Christian politics, and the Christian's ultimate allegiance to the kingdom of God, are not merely ecclesial politics.

- Israel and the church have a special heart for the poor and the oppressed. Whatever particular policies may eventuate from them, a Christian politics never loses sight of the poor, the oppressed, the outcast, and the scapegoat.
- The gospel declares one who, by teaching and example, was the "Prince of Peace." Therefore the church, in its gospel proclamation and practice, is called to peaceableness and peace-building.
- The gospel is good news and should be proclaimed as such. We learn what sin really is in light of the gospel, how damaging (deathly) separation from God/Life really is in light of the gospel. Therefore the gospel should not be proclaimed as threat or as if sin must first be demonstrated and admitted before the gospel can be heard. The gospel is first, foremost, and finally good news.

SERMONS PROCLAMATORY AND INTERROGATIVE

Once the gospel is known and accepted in its radicality—and with its political valences—the preacher has plenty to proclaim even before or without getting into the weeds of particular political policies. As our words on prudential reasoning in chapter 6 indicated, there is a difference between the gospel mandate and our prudential reasoning as to how the gospel might be "applied" or contextualized in any given case. We proclaim, repeatedly, the gospel, not our specific prudential reasoning on the gospel. If we confuse the two, we will often unnecessarily divide the church and offend our hearers in uncalled-for ways.

As the political theologian Elizabeth Phillips has recognized, the rub of preaching about politics is to do it "in ways that are not so didactic or partisan [as to] be alienating, but also not so anodyne and unthreatening as to be without challenge."[15] I am suggesting that our accent should fall on the gospel itself, which is challenging enough, politically and otherwise, and not on our derived, prudential reasonings following from and motivated by the gospel. Knowing when prudential reasoning should, judiciously and not constantly, enter into the proclamation is a determination faithful preachers will arrive at only after steeping themselves in the gospel, in prayer, in study, and in profound and ongoing relationship with their congregations. Although Christians were still arguing about it, there came a time when Christian preachers declared from the pulpit that slavery was a sin against the gospel. Although Christians were still arguing about it, there came a time when brave preachers in Germany declared Nazification a sin against the gospel. Although Christians *are* still arguing about it, there has come a time when many preachers declare the banning of women from Christian leadership a sin against the gospel. And of course there are other controversial issues today. The point is that the gospel does not, in so many words, pronounce on any of these concerns. And yet they are important. I know of no formula for when such issues present a *status confessionis,* a state where pronouncing rightly on them is required of the gospel. Yet clearly such states have come and do come to pass.

I can only repeat that we should focus mainly on the gospel as scripturally given and add that we should be aware of occasions of *status confessionis,* which we should bravely embrace, albeit with genuine fear and trembling. Beyond that, we may recall that the Bible is interrogative: it asks us questions, it puts us in question. The sermon, like the word of God, can also interrogate or question us. Recognizing this, the skillful preacher can shift from the clear, undisputed, mandatory concerns of the gospel to the specific, arguable, derived imperatives of prudential reasoning. For instance, the preacher proclaims in no uncertain terms that the gospel calls us to care for and with the poor and marginalized. But then she may shift to implied or

---

15 Elizabeth Phillips, *Apocalyptic Theopolitics: Essays and Sermons on Eschatology, Ethics, and Politics* (Eugene, OR: Cascade, 2022), xv.

explicit questions on specifics, such as these: How do *we*, in this time and place, care for and with the poor? As a congregation, how do we welcome and respect the poor? How helpful are our city and county laws and policies in serving the poor? What about our national laws and policies? These latter questions may then be picked up on in Sunday school or other formation settings, in small groups, in Bible studies—in short, in spaces where people can argue and converse and learn and implement. Such an approach would be practicable on any number of present-day issues, such as sexual ethics, gender roles, climate crisis, the advisability of specific military intervention, gun mania, and encroaching Artificial Intelligence. And it would be preferable to having the preacher pronounce, from the pulpit, on every given issue of the day. There is an inevitable and usually unwelcome element of muddling through. But muddling through is an aspect of living out of control, alive to the messy moment in which we are immersed and which, as limited and nonomniscient creatures, we can never escape. In, with, and under history, God is in control and we are not. Above all, says Käsemann, "it is necessary to listen and live knowing that the Lord never gives himself to his disciples once and for all and is always ahead of them. We do not have him in our power when we name ourselves after him."[16]

EUCHARIST AND THE GOSPEL ENJOYED

The Eucharist also is not in our power. Communicants take it with a wholly receptive attitude and bodily comportment. We kneel near the altar and offer up open palms to receive the gift of the eucharistic bread and wine. In these moments, living out of control, we acknowledge the real presence of Jesus Christ, as both the giver and gift of the feast. The Eucharist is not elitist; anyone of whatever class is welcome. Anyone who is "first" is there to serve all the others. We are sisters and brothers, everyone a citizen of the kingdom of God. Even

16 Käsemann, *Church Conflicts*, 152.

biological roles of parents and children are superseded in baptism and Eucharist—here, for example, my baptized daughter is first of all my sister in Christ. As Davor Džalto observes, "The logic of the liturgy (and, consequently, of the Church as liturgy) is remarkably anarchic."[17] So are we situated to God, as grateful receivers of God's gifts, and to one another, whom we mutually honor and in whom we see Christ.

But the Eucharist does not situate or orient us only in relation to God and to one another. It also situates us in relation to the world, physical as well as spiritual. As Geoffrey Wainwright puts it, "The bread for which we pray [in the Lord's Prayer] is *at one and the same time* both earthly bread to meet the hunger and need of the present day, and also the future bread which will satisfy the elect in the eschatological kingdom and is already given in anticipation—just as Jesus' meals with his disciples and with sinners as well as his miraculous feedings of the crowds were, in sign and reality, present experiences of the future messianic meal at which those who now hunger will be satisfied."[18] At the Eucharist, the physical elements received from the earth (wheat and grapes) are welcomed and blessed. So too is human ingenuity and creative work, which has made the wheat into bread and the grapes into wine. Thus does participation in the Eucharist imply "a commitment to the proper use of the earth's resources to the benefit of all people."[19] The Eucharist, then, situates us graciously and properly to God, to one another, to all creation. It is nothing less than doing the world as it is meant to be done.[20]

Put slightly differently, the Eucharist is training in vision. It helps us to see truthfully. We return to it frequently and constantly because we need frequent and constant corrections or adjustments to our vision, which, ever and again, is clouded by sin and the world's

---

17 Džalto, *Anarchy and the Kingdom of God*, 241.

18 Geoffrey Wainwright, *Eucharist and Eschatology* (Akron, OH: OSL, 2002), 41–42.

19 Wainwright, *Doxology*, 32.

20 For more on this theme, see Aidan Kavanagh, *On Liturgical Theology* (Collegeville, MN: Liturgical, 1984).

brokenness. The elements and actions of the Eucharist remove the cataracts of sin and death. As Wainwright remarks, "[H]umanity is still on the way to the divine kingdom. As long as this world has not given way to the next, it appears that our vision and behaviour need a periodic concentration such as the symbols of the liturgy provide. We cannot yet bear the direct and uninterrupted vision of God, and our own behaviour is correspondingly diffuse and broken, only fragmentarily in accordance with God's will. The high moments of worship are necessary in order to clarify our vision and renew us in appropriate patterns of behaviour."[21]

Like the gospel itself, which it embodies and rehearses, the Eucharist aims at transformation or transfiguration—the transformation or transfiguration of people and of all creation. As Džalto argues, "The liturgy does not deny historical, biological, and physical existence, but instead aspires to 'transfigure' it, putting it into an eschatological perspective in order for that existence to enter into communion with God."[22] Wainwright uses the same terminology to speak of the "representative role of the church and its eucharist as the *firstfruits* of the perfect society that will enjoy the feast of divine fellowship in a transfigured creation."[23]

For now, of course, all this is seen only through the eyes of faith. Christ has been resurrected; we have not yet. The kingdom has been inaugurated; it has not yet been consummated. But, says Wainwright,

the present invisibility of the divine glory is to be understood positively because it is due to God's willingness that people should come freely to acknowledge his sovereignty and therefore to *enjoy* his kingdom. The divine glory which is the mark of God's presence and rule must always be on the point of breaking through into visibility, for God is *God*, and if he refrains from the incontestable establishment of his universal rule, it is because he gives people time to hear the gospel of

---

21 Wainwright, *Doxology*, 405.

22 Džalto, *Anarchy and the Kingdom of God*, 183.

23 Wainwright, *Eucharist and Eschatology*, 51.

Jesus Christ, to seize its promise in hope, to let their lives be shaped by his transforming presence, and to order their daily actions in the world according to the rule of God.[24]

In this regard, Wainwright speaks of the "polarities of hiddenness and visibility" as "contestability and incontestability."[25] As I argued in this book's early chapters, God wants not abject, forced servility with God's creation, but instead loving relationship. God wants us not simply to acknowledge the kingdom but to *enjoy* it. So now, on this side of the eschaton, the gospel and its entailments remain contestable. They can be debated, ignored, even refused. And that is God's will. We as followers of Jesus are congruently called not to force or impose the gospel on others. We are not to manipulate, con, or intimidate them. Our witness instead is to live out of control and to enjoy the kingdom come and coming—so vividly, truthfully, excitingly, and delightfully that others might wish to join us.

---

24 Wainwright, *Eucharist and Eschatology*, 152.
25 Wainwright, *Eucharist and Eschatology*, 183.

CHAPTER EIGHT

Friendship

On the night before his death, according to the Gospel of John, Jesus declares his disciples his friends. He gives his great commandment, "that you love one another as I have loved you" (John 15:12). He tells them that one can have no greater love than to lay down his life for his friends, an act to which he has already committed himself. Then he tells them, "I do not call you servants any longer, because the servant does not know what the master is doing; but I have called you friends, because I have made known to you everything that I have heard from my Father" (15:15).

This text tells us something about deep friendship and about discipleship. In a deep friendship there are few if any secrets. Close friends know one another profoundly, not just in terms of strengths but in terms of weaknesses and wounds. They willingly reveal themselves to one another. In the Gospel of John, Jesus offers deep friendship to the disciples. He is ready to lay down his life for them. And he keeps no secrets from them about what he has learned from his Father.

Masters may withhold secrets from their servants (and vice versa), but here Jesus shares intimate knowledge. As the prolific New Testament scholar Craig Keener notes, "Under Jewish law, a slave could not inherit . . . unless the will freed the slave or granted him 'all' his master's goods. . . . There would be no point in Jesus promising to share his words or goods with the disciples unless they were friends and not slaves."[1]

Secrets are powerful and can grant a degree of control over another. Consider their role as capital in espionage. Or, in a more mundane environment, think of a situation in which you and I know a woman to which we are both romantically drawn. I learn from one of her confiding girlfriends that the woman of interest is attracted to you. Capitalizing on the power of secreted information, I choose to keep this knowledge from you while I pursue the woman. My secret gives me control. Similarly, consider a workplace situation. I learn our boss is passionately committed to a certain course of action while you are writing a report recommending the opposite course. To your benefit, I might share that knowledge with you. But in this case, I keep it secret so that I might better curry the boss's favor and perhaps get a leg up on a promotion for which we are both competing. Again, a secret can give advantage and control.

Yet Jesus does not keep secrets; he shares the words of life, what he knows from this Father. He does not traffic in advantage or clandestine control. He lives out of control and calls his followers to a similar way of life. He makes the disciples his friends and not simply his slaves, and his refusal to hide or keep secrets, as friends do not do, suggests one way friendship is a school for living out of control.

FRIENDSHIP AS A SCHOOL FOR LIVING OUT OF CONTROL

Now in my sixties, when I look back on a life blessed with friendships, many of them long and close, I can see that I could never have predicted the particular people who have become my friends. People of all sorts are my friends. Some friendships I initiated. In other cases another took the initiative and came into my life out of the blue. There were people I would have liked to have been friends with, but

1 Craig S. Keener, *The Gospel of John: A Commentary* (Grand Rapids: Baker Academic, 2003), 1013.

it never quite "took." There were (and are) many I would never have imagined or predicted as friends—because we were quite different, or came from different stations in life, or we even at first disliked each other. Such friendships came as surprises and have brought surprises with them all along the way. Friends resonate—they strike a mutual chord—but they are never identical to me. And the friendships that have lasted have done so in part because we two friends were willing to live out of control, to let the other be himself or herself.

All this points to another way in which friendship can be a school for living out of control. In theological terms, friends are a gift from God. In one sense, we choose our friends and they choose us. But in another sense, God has brought people into our lives that we never would have predicted or managed simply on our own devices. So, says the theologian of friendship Paul Wadell, "From first to last, these [Christian friendships, between two striving together toward the kingdom of God], are gifts of God. We cannot choose them, but we can receive them. We cannot control them, but we can be redeemed through them."[2]

Wadell's last sentence bears emphasis. To live as friends is to live out of control of our friends. In a deep friendship, we are committed to another person—the whole person, with all her virtues and flaws, all her fine points and foibles. We have probably never taken formal vows to one another, but in a deep friendship it is understood at a profound level that we intend to be there for one another, till death do us part. It is exactly this kind of commitment that leaves us vulnerable and out of control. As the philosopher Gary Chartier remarks, the development and direction of a friendship is "not subject to our wills and thus place[s] our own well-being outside our control."[3] It is a matter of trust—trust not that my friend will act and be exactly as I would like, but that my friend really has my own well-being at heart. Here is how the philosopher Todd May puts it: "Trust is not

---

2 Paul J. Wadell, *Friendship and the Moral Life* (Notre Dame, IN: University of Notre Dame Press, 1989), 98.

3 Gary Chartier, *Understanding Friendship: On the Moral, Political, and Spiritual Meaning of Love* (Minneapolis: Fortress, 2022), 35.

the calculation that the friend will act in certain ways. It is instead placing oneself in the hands of the friend. It is to let loose (without entirely abandoning) the grip of one's own cognitive orientation toward the world in favor of another's. . . . To trust a close friend is not to think that it is likely that she will not lead one astray; it is to be in a space where that thought doesn't arise, because one has put herself at her friend's disposal."[4] Such nonmanipulative and deep trust enables Wadell to say, rightly, "We cannot control [our friends], but we can be redeemed through them." As May says, friends in trust put themselves at one another's "disposal."

Someone once told me she chose her local church in light of whom she wants to bury her. I take it she was thinking about constancy and certainly trust. "Someday," she was saying, "I will die and be maximally out of control. It will then be up to others to literally dispose of my body, hopefully with dignity and grace and loving care." Friendships might be accepted and embraced on the same basis: whom do you want to bury you? Those are the persons to whom you should put yourself at the disposal.

At any event, when we put ourselves at the disposal of friends, we enter uncharted and unchartable territory. Friendships surprisingly (and as gifts) come into being, and they grow "in unstructured, unplanned, and seemingly unmanageable ways."[5] Friends may literally take us to new places, as they move to a new city or country and we go there to visit. Their jobs may change or develop in novel directions, so that they bring new questions and challenges. They may embrace a different philosophy of life and push us to consider matters we had never before dreamed of. They may contract a disease or fall ill with cancer or begin to suffer Parkinson's or dementia, thus thrusting us into whole new worlds of discourses and experiences. They may fail morally, even embark on criminal activity, or suffer substance addiction. Since friendships are contingent in these senses, there is no end to the ways they may surprise us and put us

---

4 Todd May, *Friendship in an Age of Economics: Resisting the Forces of Neoliberalism* (Lanham, MD: Lexington, 2012), 114.

5 Chartier, *Understanding Friendship*, 47.

out of control. As Chartier says, "Even when a friend behaves well, of course, we may lose her—on the battlefield, on the highway, in the hospital, in an easy chair. What will happen to a friend, and so to a friendship, lies outside our control."[6]

In all the ways we have been discussing, friendship is a school for living out of control. So the church can learn and benefit from friendship, both in its midst and outside it. Especially in a fragmented and desperately lonely society, the church has much to offer by way of friendship. This is not to say all the members of a local church must be one another's close or deep friends—that would be unrealistic and cultish. It is to say that the church should be a place where members are friendly to one another, and where some deep friendships can be initiated and sustained. The church, after all, is all about trust (faith) in God and in one another. Jesus calls us to "love one another as I have loved you." Let the church be a space and time where people benefit from friendship and learn transferable skills and capacities to be taken out into the surrounding world, living out of control. Says Chartier, "[I]f people can learn in church how to value others in their particularity, they will have discovered something important about how to be friends. A church that recognizes God as revealed in the crucifixion of Jesus must be alert to the value of nondomination, the value of acknowledging otherness even when it's disturbing and unsettling and threatening."[7]

FRIENDSHIP AND POLITICS

But are friendships political? In some respects, yes; in other respects, not so much if at all. Remember that through these pages we have considered different forms and contexts of politics: prefigurative politics, anarchical politics, gospel politics, and governmental politics.

Christian prefigurative politics perform (if only in part) the world today that we want or expect tomorrow. The ventures undertaken in

6 Chartier, *Understanding Friendship*, 48.
7 Chartier, *Understanding Friendship*, 168.

prefigurative politics can often be motivated, animated, and strengthened by shared friendships. When Christians care together for the sick, visit prisoners, or operate soup kitchens, they often develop friendships in the course of such undertakings. Friendships, following conversations about shared concerns, may even lead to the initiation of these ventures. Perhaps, for instance, a Bible study group reads of Jesus's concern for prisoners, sees a need in their city or county, and starts a visitation program. And friendships may sustain prefigurative politics as they meet obstacles, friend encouraging and helping friend.

As for anarchical politics, they too may be animated and sustained by friendship. It has been said, "Friendship is outside the reach of the law; it produces its own laws, it lacks a formalized status, and it is in this sense an anarchic form of relating."[8] To the degree friendship is anarchic, it helps us as Christians to remember and become more skilled in our own, eschatologically based anarchic tendencies. As friendships take us in surprising directions, they may open up new worlds and ways of thought and imagination. They remind us, even when we don't necessarily want to be reminded, that what *is*, is not necessarily what *ought* to be. Because different friends experience different kinds and degrees of sensitivities, my friend's sensitivity may open my eyes to an injustice or need I had overlooked.

In addition, and related to the anarchical tendency, though friends need not necessarily be dissenters from the wider society, "there is a natural fit between friendship and dissent."[9] As Chartier argues, friendships and friendship circles "offer people settings in which they can express dissenting views as well as the confidence to voice those views publicly. This need not be because the friends share a dissenter's views; what matters is that they are willing to accept her."[10] Since I know my friends accept me, even if they disagree with certain of my views, I can take courage to be me and speak out on a controversial issue. So friendships can bolster the anarchic tendency. As Chartier

---

8 Mihalis Mentinis, quoted in Chartier, *Understanding Friendship*, 12n35.

9 Chartier, *Understanding Friendship*, 164.

10 Chartier, *Understanding Friendship*, 164.

says, "In virtue of its relative independence and its capacity to serve as a counterweight to other social forces, the friendship group can turn out to be countercultural, even potentially revolutionary, even if it didn't form initially because its members were political dissenters or in order to encourage dissent."[11]

As pastoral theologian Anne-Marie Ellithorpe notes, Martin Luther King Jr. did not fight for civil rights alone. Friends with him—providing courage and encouragement, offering ideas and strategies, taking blows alongside him—included John Lewis, James Lawson, Andrew Young, C. T. Vivian, and Abraham Joshua Heschel. Friendship was also vital to Nelson Mandela and others in the struggle against South African apartheid. And the liberation theologian Gustavo Guttiérrez advocated for solidarity with the poor through friendships with them.[12]

Aside from its direct, internal connection to prefigurative and anarchical politics, friendship can inform politics of all sorts, and hone transferable skills that can be put to work even (if not especially) in governmental political settings. Most broadly, friendship can serve such politics by helping us learn how to accept and respect others as others. We can learn how to accept diversity in political others by accepting diversity in our friends. In friendship we learn skills of engaging others with empathy, courtesy, "and in a manner marked by openness to discovery, self-disclosure, and, indeed, the possibility of change-inducing realization. Friendship can function as a school for this kind of conversation." Friendship groups also hone skills in being open to alternative views, vulnerable conversation, and learning how to "negotiate difference and resolve challenges

---

11 Chartier, *Understanding Friendship*, 164–165.

12 Anne-Marie Ellithorpe, *Towards Friendship-Shaped Communities: A Practical Theology of Friendship* (Oxford: Wiley Blackwell, 2022), 35. Earlier, the French Catholic philosopher Jacques Maritain emphasized the importance of friendships with the poor: "Before 'doing good' *to* them, and working *for* their benefit, we must choose to exist *with* them and to suffer with them, to make their pain and destiny our own." Cited in Brenna Moore, *Kindred Spirits: Friendship and Resistance at the Edges of Modern Catholicism* (Chicago: University of Chicago Press, 2021), 54.

related to power." In short, "We discover in the practice of friendship metaphors and analogies which we can bring to bear to inform our public and [governmental] political activity."[13]

FRIENDSHIP, GOSPEL POLITICS, GOVERNMENTAL POLITICS, AND A BROTHERLY SALUTE

As I hope chapter 7 made clear, there is a distinction between the gospel politics and governmental politics. Gospel politics are a given for all Christians, and at least rough agreement on central gospel mandates is not only possible but achievable. Governmental politics and policies, on the other hand, are derived and arrived at by one (or two, or more) steps of prudential judgment and discernment. On these Christians can and very often do disagree. What is key is not to confuse or identify these prudential judgments with the gospel. To flesh this out in the current context—one in which the US is riven and democracy has been weakened—I want to dwell on my relationship with my brother.

Kerry and I are deep friends. We share not only parents and a common place of upbringing but a genuine respect and affection for one another. We also share a common faith. In this, though he is the younger, Kerry has often taken the initiative. It was he who, as an early teenager, decided to be baptized. Our mother thought the two of us should be baptized on the same occasion, so I followed his lead. A few years later, after a revival of sorts, it was Kerry who approached me to express love and respect, as well as forgiveness concerning our (typical) sibling rivalry and resentments, enabling the deepening of our relationship.[14] Since then both of us have continued in the faith and consistent discipleship. Thus I stand with

---

13 Chartier, *Understanding Friendship*, 161, 191, 162.

14 A "lay witness mission," to be precise. These intense weekend gatherings had laypeople stay in the homes of church members at the church receiving the mission, while worship periods focused on lay testimonies, much singing, and shared meals.

my brother in blood who is first of all a brother in baptism and a true friend in the gospel.

We share much, then, but our views on governmental politics are decidedly different. We argued these politics for decades, and neither of us fundamentally changed the other's mind. Now we mostly talk about other things. We are, of course, both born of the same parents. We both grew up in the same rural Oklahoma community and attended the same undergraduate university. What accounts for our profound governmental political differences? Part of it, I suppose, goes down to deeply ingrained temperamental differences—and any parent can tell you one child's temperament and personality can differ dramatically from another's. A second part goes down to innate abilities. My brother was more practical, competent, and comfortable on the farm than I was. He developed mechanical affinities while I developed literary and artistic interests. Yet another aspect was our undergraduate schooling. I trained as a journalist and political scientist. Kerry trained as a mechanical and aerospace engineer. This is not to say all journalists are "liberal" and all engineers are "conservative." But many journalists do skew "liberal" and engineers can skew "conservative." These and other differences contribute to our disagreed prudential viewpoints on governmental politics. Some of them are almost accidental—or at least they are beyond our easy self-awareness and close control.

But we both live our lives in light of the gospel and ultimate allegiance to Jesus Christ. We both base our communal lives in the church. In this we are as one. And over the years, our friendship has deepened. We partnered, with our sister, to care for our elderly mother suffering from dementia. We both pray and care for the other's growing families. We talk on the phone weekly and have much to say, though—again—rarely about governmental politics.

This reality or rationale extends beyond my relationship with my brother. I thank God for friends inside and outside the church who largely agree with my prudential discernments on governmental politics. But no less, and in some ways more, I thank God for those friends who disagree. They keep me honest. They remind me not to confuse my highest governmental political goals with the arrival of the kingdom of God in its fullness. And in our joy together they remind me that there is more to life than governmental politics—so much more.

All told, then, friendship can contribute to change on multiple political levels. And it brings many other riches besides.

CHAPTER NINE

Resonance

Friends resonate. The buttery sunlight before dusk resonates. A dog or cat in the lap resonates. The smell of coffee in the morning resonates. A flowing mountain river resonates. A lake or an ocean with its lapping waves resonates. The rolling prairie under a starry sky resonates. A campfire on a chilly night resonates. Gracious ritual, observed with dignity, resonates. The embrace of a lover resonates.

Resonance can occur through any or all of our senses. It is a relationship, a response-able relationship, between two parties. To better appreciate it, we may attend to it in its most literal presentation, namely that of sound and especially of music. Strike a tuning fork and a nearby tuning fork will vibrate and itself sound. Pluck one string on a guitar and other strings will hum. Thus when two musical notes are sounded together, they do not "stand" or sound separately, alongside one another, but they interpenetrate each other—while still being heard as two distinct notes. Music occurs because of what is called "sympathetic resonance." As the theologian and musician Jeremy Begbie explains,

> [Resonance] is clearly not a case of mutual diminution: rather, the *more* the lower string sounds, the *more* the upper string sounds. The tones we hear are not in competition, nor do they simply allow each other room. The lower sound establishes the upper, frees it to be itself, enhances it, without compromising its

own integrity. Moreover, when certain other strings are opened up alongside these strings—for example, to make an extended major chord—we will hear those strings coming to life.[1]

Notice several features of this comment, true (I suggest) not just of music but of resonance in general. First, the sounding strings do not diminish but actually enhance one another. Second, while each string retains its own "identity" or integrity, it does not compete with or merely "make room" for others. Third, each string or party to resonance is freed to be itself by the sounding of others. And fourth, it is shareable, it spreads and enriches, cascading into chords where all strings come to life.

When we move resonance from the literal, aural level to the metaphorical level encompassing a variety of relationships, and including other senses in addition to hearing, we see the same phenomena at work. A resonant relationship enhances rather than diminishes the parties to it. We speak of a person "coming to life" in a vital romance or friendship. Yet a resonant relationship does not destroy or lessen the identity or integrity of each "individual" entering into it. In fact, we may say that Jack is "most himself" when he is with Mary, or when he is fishing or golfing. And resonant relationships are shareable and enriched by others' enjoyment. Our first impulse, on chancing upon a beautiful painting or taking in a sunrise, is to enlist others to enjoy these things too. Somehow their shared enjoyment does not lessen but increases our own enjoyment.

To Begbie's evocations, I want to add a summary factor. Resonance, to be experienced, requires us to be out of control.

RESONANCE OUT OF OUR CONTROL

A resonant and deep friendship, as we saw in chapter 8, entails letting my friend be an other, truly herself. To make a friend strictly

---

1 Quoted in Wirzba, *This Sacred Life*, 184.

a reflection of myself, I reduce friendship to puppetry or ventrilo-
quism, an echo of myself. Resonance, as distinct from a mere echo,
demands that each friend be allowed to speak with her own voice. As
the sociologist Hartmut Rosa puts it, "An echo lacks its own voice . . .
What resounds in an echo is never a response, but only ever oneself."
Furthermore, in friendship we are talking about a true other, one
who may at times irritate, upset, or contradict me. "Not blind agreement, but the ability and willingness to contradict is a prerequisite
of any resonant relationship, as this is what makes it possible for the
subject to find in the world a response that amounts to more than
an echo," says Rosa.[2] So the resonance of a true friendship depends
on my living out of control of my friend. The same may be said of
other resonant relationships or experiences. The resonant sun is out
of my control—I must wait for its rising or setting and any resonant
effects they may produce. And I suppose many a wedding has been
marred by the attempt to make it "perfect," to control every detail
and aspect of its unfolding. At some point, to enjoy a resonant wedding, the bride and groom must relax control and simply live in each
successive moment.

Now, this is not to say resonance cannot be prepared for, or that
conditions for its experience may not entail considerable work beforehand and even during the experience. Enduring resonant friendships
entail some planning and coordination of calendars, as well as other
ongoing effort. Musicians put lifetimes of practice behind the concert that resonantly sweeps me away. Or consider the celebration of
the Eucharist. In my Episcopal tradition, where the celebration is
fairly elaborate, each Eucharist requires many hands and hours of
application, before and during. The altar guild beforehand sets the
altar linens, prepares candles, washes and presents cup and paten,
decants wine, bakes bread. The celebration itself requires the training
and participation of clergy and acolytes. The lay participants play
their own prepared roles, reciting corporate prayers and responding

---

2 Hartmut Rosa, *Resonance: A Sociology of Our Relationship to the World*
(Cambridge: Polity, 2019), 167, 191, with emphasis deleted in each case.

appropriately at set times. A slapdash Eucharist, without all this effort, would be more chaos than celebration.

Yet at other times resonance comes unbidden, as if out of the blue. We have not planned or looked for it but it serendipitously strikes. One day the famous monk Thomas Merton was casually walking the streets of Louisville, Kentucky. "At the corner of Fourth and Walnut, in the center of the shopping district," he writes, "I was suddenly overwhelmed with the realization that I loved all these people, that they were mine and I theirs, that we could not be alien to one another even though we were total strangers. It was like waking from a dream of separateness, of spurious self-isolation." Merton experienced such "relief" and joy that he "almost laughed out loud."[3] It was a pristine instance of resonance. "Self-isolation" and alienation melted away— the "dream of separateness" faded. Merton profoundly resonated with the "total strangers" surrounding him.

So resonance may altogether surprise, or it may be something for which we have prepared and hoped, laying out the conditions for it. Even in the latter case, however, it occurs outside our control. The best, most thorough preparations do not always result in resonance. The bride who cannot relax into the moment will never enjoy her wedding. The man stewing in anger will not resonate at the eucharistic altar. In fact, it is axiomatic: if we insist on remaining in control, on producing resonance at will, it will never come.

FROM A RESONANT TO A MUTE UNIVERSE

It may be argued that the world was once a profoundly resonant place. Human selves were not "buffered," as the philosopher Charles Taylor puts it, but were open to and interpenetrated by a lively universe populated with angels and demons, magic, a "great chain of being."[4]

---

3 Thomas Merton, *Conjectures of a Guilty Bystander* (New York: Image, 1966), 153–154.

4 Charles Taylor, *A Secular Age* (Cambridge, MA: The Belknap Press of Harvard University Press, 2007), 37–42 and throughout.

Even as late as the nineteenth century, the poet William Blake could question himself that at the sun's rising, did he not see merely "a round Disk of fire somewhat like a Guinea"? He answered urgently and ecstatically, "O no no I see an Innumerable company of the Heavenly host crying Holy Holy Holy is the Lord God Almighty."[5] The philosophers Landon Loftin and Max Leyf observe that Blake was not denying science or solar astrophysics. Nor was he indulging in mere metaphor. Rather, Blake was looking through the corporeal to the spiritual reality, just as he would look *through* a window and not simply *at* its glass. For Blake, say Loftin and Leyf, the sun was not "merely a convenient metaphor for the glory of God," but "a real expression of such, just as an unconscious smile was not simile but a real expression of human happiness."[6]

That we today do not live in such richly a resonant world is evidenced by the stretch or effort required of us to look at (and through) the sun and see something more than a "round Disk of fire somewhat like a Guinea." It is evidenced by our alienation from others and rampant loneliness. It is evidenced by our hostility to governmental politics and a global political economy that threatens not to include or incorporate us, to our good, but to overwhelm us. Helmut Rosa points to a host of other signs that we are starved for resonance. Consider the growing massage and touch industries, heavy metal concerts, and gross media violence and pornography. "All these phenomena," remarks Rosa, "may reflect nothing other than various attempts to re-establish resonance between self and world, to make self and world sensitive to each other again." The boom in "organic," "natural," "non-processed foods" expresses a "longing for a different, non-alienating relationship to this world." Meanwhile, esoteric New Age spiritualities brim with a longing for "occult resonant relationships (between fate and the stars; stones, herbs, and organs; earlier and later experiences of incarnations; present and absent people,

---

5 William Blake, *The Complete Poetry and Prose of William Blake* (New York: Anchor, 1988), 565–566.

6 Landon Loftin and Max Leyf, *What Barfield Thought: An Introduction to the Work of Owen Barfield* (Eugene, OR: Cascade, 2023), 107.

the living and the dead, etc.)." And late modernity's obsession with the body can "well be understood as indicating a loss of resonant physical relationships to the world."[7]

There are various causes for diminished resonance, but the one that interests me here is the modern mania for control. To be sure, there are felicitous occasions for control and objectification. I am glad my surgeon, for example, objectifies my body and organs when she calmly and disinterestedly plies the knife. And I like my airline pilot quite calculatedly attending to his gauges and instruments while not getting lost in mystical rhapsodies about the sun or stars outside his window. But modernity features "an *incessant* desire to make the world engineerable, predictable, available, accessible, disposable . . . *in all its aspects.*"[8] The modern, controlling deportment is a disposition "toward individual segments of the world . . . marked by an attitude of determination, domination, transformation, and conquest."[9] In fact, "The driving cultural force of that form of life we call 'modern' is the idea, the hope and desire, that we can make the world controllable. Yet it is only in encountering the uncontrollable that we really experience the world. Only then do we feel touched, moved, alive. A world that is fully known, in which everything has been planned and mastered, would be a dead world."[10] At the least, in our aversion to living out of control, we inhabit a "mute universe."[11]

And what is the result of inhabiting a "mute universe"? Norman Wirzba answers, "[Resonant] relationships happen when people feel that they are alive to others and that the world welcomes their presence and engagement. When the relations between self and world no longer 'vibrate,' that is, when they can no longer *feel* the lives of others within themselves, it is likely that people will become unhappy, perhaps even depressed and aggressive, because the world registers

---

7 Rosa, *Resonance*, 55, 61, 87.

8 Hartmut Rosa, *The Uncontrollability of the World* (Cambridge: Polity, 2020), viii, emphasis added.

9 Rosa, *Resonance*, 13.

10 Rosa, *Uncontrollability of the World*, 2, emphasis deleted.

11 Rosa, *Resonance*, 225.

as a bleak and alien place, and one experiences oneself as numb, abandoned, or uninspired."[12]

RECOVERING THE CONDITIONS FOR RESONANCE

As we have seen, resonance cannot be fabricated. There is no technology or formula for producing it. In fact, one sure way to block resonance is to try to force it. However, we can be more or less open to resonance. We can, as in preparation for a eucharistic celebration, set conditions more rather than less propitious for resonance.

In terms of prefigurative politics, the church might be a place where deep friendships are likely to form. It might be a people who recognize the value and virtue of living out of control and put that into practice in many—even most—aspects of life. It might be a space where the gospel is proclaimed and embodied, and the gospel as truly good news—the healing of estrangement between ourselves and God, ourselves and others, and ourselves and creation—will certainly resonate. It might be a place where people are formed in responsibility as response-ability, where people learn to engage others and the rest of creation receptively and interactively. In its singing, its most literally resonant practice, the church can glimpse and reveal a degree of harmony and shared joy that can spill over into life at large. Rosa adds, "[Formation] in the sense of resonance theory . . . is aimed not at cultivating either the world or the self, but rather at cultivating relationships to the world. The goal is not refinement of the individualistic or atomistic self, nor disengaged mastery of the world, but rather opening up and establishing axes of resonance. Children [and disciples] are not vessels to be filled, but torches to be lit."[13] So, let "Disciples are not vessels to be filled, but torches to be lit" be the church's resonant mantra.

---

12 Wirzba, *This Sacred Life*, 236.

13 Rosa, *Resonance*, 241. I have substituted the word *formation* for *education* at the beginning of the sentence.

We can look to Rosa for other conditions of resonance. The first, which we have emphasized already, is the necessary inaccessibility of resonance. We cannot force it; we must let go and be open to it. The second concerns resonance and time. "Looking at the clock always signals an interruption, if not the end, of a resonant experience," notes Rosa.[14] In the midst of resonance, time is suspended. Chronological, linear experience of time is transcended. Caught up in an enthralling novel, we may look at the clock and realize we missed lunchtime. "Time flies when you're having (resonant) fun." Friends may fall into engrossing conversation and suddenly realize two hours have passed.

Opening time to resonance entails not being obsessed with hurry and a sense of urgency to move on to the next thing. This condition might be helped by something so simple as not wearing a watch to corporate worship. It definitely necessitates setting aside time to make space for resonance. Rosa notes that resonance of a deep sort is often time intensive. "A person who picks up a violin only once will not have a resonant experience with it, nor will someone who picks up *The Magic Mountain* but reads only the blurb—that is, unless they have already established an axis of resonance to Thomas Mann or to literature. In the same way, fleeting acquaintances can be precisely that: mere acquaintants, but not friendships in the sense of a relation of resonance . . ."[15]

A second condition of resonance is basic trust, in others and in the world. We will not find resonance with people we deeply distrust. And if the world is perceived as mute or hostile, there can be little resonance with it. Christian trust is built on faith in a God of grace and love, working for the best of God's creation. Julian of Norwich's epigram—"All will be well and all will be well and all manner of thing will be well"—expresses an eschatological hope that a gracious God will not abandon God's creation, and will strive with and for it until its ultimate good is realized. This grounds an attitude of trust in and

14 Rosa, *Resonance,* 416.
15 Rosa, *Resonance,* 416, emphasis deleted.

openness to the world. Meanwhile, as concerns relations with other people, Christ calls the disciple to look out for the good and felicity of the other. "Outdo one another in showing honor," exhorts the Apostle Paul (Rom 12:10). A community built on these commands and exhortations will be one in which people have one another's back, one in which basic trust is a gift and a given.

Of course, trust is imperfect in a world or church before the eschaton. In this time between the times, the world sometimes lashes out, as with wildfires and tornadoes, or through an unjust political system. And people, including friends, will sometimes fail us—and even if friends do not fail us, they will fall ill or die. So, because resonance requires vulnerability and we live in an imperfect world, we must be willing to face and endure suffering. As Rosa says, "A person who is willing to be touched and affected must also be willing to be hurt."[16] Consequently, a people open to resonance must live with trust but also be cleareyed in facing the fact that trust will not always be repaid. Again, such a people will dare to suffer, though they need not invite it.

These three conditions for openness to resonance—the willingness to live out of control, taking time, and learning trust while admitting suffering—are attitudes and deportments that can be cultivated within and by the church. They play into the church's prefigurative politics. But what about governmental politics? It can be argued that democracy is the most potentially resonant form of governmental politics known or available to us. Democracy, after all, elicits the vital participation of all citizens, and not just the lopsided, top-down involvement of a monarch, dictator, or totalitarian oligarchy. Democracy (ideally) gives all citizens a voice, whereas these other forms of government allow only for an echo of the dominant "leader" or party. Rosa robustly supports democracy: "Democratic politics . . . is an indispensable element for appropriating, or, better, adaptively transforming the world."[17]

---

16 Rosa, *Resonance*, 416.

17 Rosa, *Resonance,* 39, emphasis deleted.

The current crisis of democracy, Rosa believes, is that "it no longer seems to be responsive to citizens" and "is no longer a 'sphere of resonance.'" He suggests that democracy at its best is a kind of music. "We speak not only of voices, but of harmony, dissonance, orchestration, discord, working in concert, etc." Strengthening democracy means recognizing its resonant and musical potential—and recognizing that it is much larger than legislation and the conflict of interests. "Democracy here no longer denotes merely nor even primarily the negotiation and settlement of legal claims and conflicts of interest but rather refers to an ongoing process of becoming more sensitive to a variety of voices in the sense of perspectives, modes of existence, and relationships to the world."[18]

We might shore up and revitalize democracy by working for policies that address the dangerously extreme inequality of our society, by resisting the reduction of citizens to harshly competing entrepreneurs their whole lives, and by reducing the precarity enveloping vast numbers of citizens (in a word, resisting neoliberalism). We might also enact a "rule of law" that the powerful cannot elude or manipulate to their advantage, and by continuing to work against racism, white supremacy, and patriarchy. Rosa himself points to the (prefigurative?) "experimental practices of the sharing economy or of transition towns," to "creative new cooperatives and communities," to spaces and organizations "wherever citizens are reappropriating the infrastructure and institutions of energy supply, buying them back from the private market as a community."[19]

Finally, while remaining clear-eyed and unsentimental, we might work among ourselves to avoid the coruscating cynicism and (often faux) outrage so prevalent in our current politics. "Cynical *laughing at* and *shouting against* are not only undemocratic or non-democratic forms of expression, they also indicate repulsive mode of relation, demonstrating that the resonant wire between citizens and politics has been severed," says Rosa. What's more,

---

18 Rosa, *Resonance*, 42 (emphasis deleted), 217, 218.
19 Rosa, *Resonance*, 225, emphasis deleted.

"there appears to be an inverse relationship between a political move-ment's intensity of outrage and its sensitivity to resonance (which demands contradiction)."[20] The Christian caring for resonance and for democracy might at the least forgo execrable and demeaning language and conduct on the internet, through other media, and in face-to-face encounters.

WISDOM, ATTUNEMENT, AND PRAYER

As we near the conclusion of this chapter and book, I want to intro-duce one more interlocutor: the erudite Baptist theologian Paul Fid-des. He ruminates suggestively on the Hebrew wisdom tradition and how it calls us to use thought and imagination not "for the sake of controlling other things and people," but for respecting and mak-ing adaptive contact with the world. This stance to the world "is associated with terms such as 'embodiment,' 'connectedness,' and 'participation'"—and, I might add, "resonance." Says Fiddes, "A guid-ing thread is the sense that wisdom is about living in tune with the world in which we are placed, in all its differences and otherness." Hebrew wisdom "thus lays stress on the flourishing of the human self in its interconnection to other persons and the natural world."[21]

In the Bible's wisdom literature (including the Psalms, Proverbs, and Job), there is confidence that the wise person can observe nature and social life and learn something of their rhythms and ways. But, says Fiddes, "Alongside confidence there is a strong note of caution. For all the hard discipline, the teacher of wisdom was prepared to recognize an element of the unpredictable in all calculations: there are unknown factors which the wise person must reckon with. The multiplicity and variety of the world order with which the wise are dealing can never be completely mastered, and always have a capacity

---

20 Rosa, *Resonance,* 222 (emphasis in original) and 225 (emphasis deleted).

21 Paul S. Fiddes, *Seeing the World and Knowing God: Hebrew Wisdom and Christian Doctrine in a Late-Modern Context* (Oxford: Oxford University Press, 2013), 4, 15.

to surprise." In other words, the wise person recognizes that she significantly lives out of control. For Fiddes reading the wisdom tradition, "The elusiveness of the physical world lies in its sheer extent, and also in its complexity."[22] In this connection he cites as an example Proverbs 30:18–19: "Three things are too wonderful for me; four I do not understand: the way of an eagle in the sky, the way of a snake on a rock, the way of a ship on the high seas, and the way of a man with a girl."

Human wisdom contrasts with God's wisdom. Human wisdom "is limited by the scope of its material—its diversity, multiplicity, and complexity that can never be fully grasped by human minds." On the other hand, "God has possession of wisdom because he has a grasp of all the complexities of the world. Every element and item in the whole range of nature [and social life] lies open to his observation, and he can therefore steer his way through creation with complete certainty." In summary, "Here is the heart of the riddle: God knows wisdom because God knows the world in its inexhaustibility, while human beings know wisdom in a lesser way because they are limited in knowing the world." Thus Proverbs 30:1–4: "I have not learned wisdom . . . not ascended to heaven and come down . . . not grasped the wind in the hollow of my hand . . . not wrapped up the waters in a garment . . . not established the ends of the earth."[23]

In sum, human wisdom is powerful and respectable, but it does not leave us in control, certainly not in control as God can exercise it. What we can best and most fortuitously attempt is not conquest, dominance, and utter mastery but what Rosa calls resonance, or what Fiddes describes as attunement—"sympathetic engagement with the wisdom immanent in the world" and available to human knowing. As Fiddes quotes Jeremy Begbie, "wisdom is directed towards a life-style thoroughly 'in tune' with God . . . that resonates aptly with the Creator's intentions for us and the world." And more, even

---

22 Fiddes, *Seeing the World and Knowing God*, both quotes at 97.

23 Fiddes, *Seeing the World and Knowing God*, 110 (emphasis deleted), 236, 240.

more wonderfully, we can know (returning to Fiddes) that "God sets the standard pitch in Jesus Christ, and we are attuned through contemplating this revelation in the Gospels." Finally, in this vein, "Observing an object or another person without trying to control them is a sharing in the flow of love in the triune life of God."[24]

A central Christian practice for attunement with God and God's ways is prayer. In prayer we posture our bodies so as to embody optimally living out of control. We place our hands in our lap or fold them or lift them with open, empty palms. Our hands are our primary instruments for touching, grasping, or manipulating the world. When we still, fold, and/or open our hands, we thus suspend our instrumental control of the world. If we close our eyes as well, we suspend the sense that enables us to see, anticipate, and direct the world. Sometimes we kneel in prayer, signaling our surrender, adopting a posture not of fight or flight but of vulnerability and receptiveness.

In prayer we listen and we speak our thanks, praise, confessions, petitions, or intercessions. Two voices are allowed or elicited: that of God and of ourselves. Our gracious God, as the Psalms and other biblical texts demonstrate, allows us freedom to address God boldly, and even to argue and remonstrate with God. Accordingly, prayer invites true resonance—there are two voices, and we are not expected to merely echo God's voice. All said, then, through its posturing and basic attitude, prayer "in its very concept is designed to produce 'deep resonance.'"[25]

To this we might add the Christian emphasis on grace and the gifts of God. Grace is not earned, compelled, or demanded. God gives grace freely, and nothing about it, neither its reception nor its enduring character, has anything to do with human control. Rather, it is rooted in an attitude of gratitude, openness, and receptiveness, to which the human can contribute only her attunement to God

---

24 Fiddes, *Seeing the World and Knowing God*, 375, 376, 393.

25 Rosa, *Resonance*, 261.

and acceptance of God's gift.[26] In the light of resonance theory, the Apostle Paul's enigmatic advice to "pray without ceasing" (1 Thess 5:17) might be read as exhortation to let the attitude and posturing of formal prayer spill over into and suffuse all of life. Paul may be urging us to let formal prayer train us so as to be optimally open in every moment to the possibility of resonance with God, God's world, and other persons. In short, to "pray without ceasing" may be a call to live out of control.

---

26 See Rosa, *Uncontrollability of the World*, 59.

Bibliography

Barth, Karl. *Church Dogmatics* IV/1. Translated by G. W. Bromiley. Edinburgh: T. & T. Clark, 1956.

———. *Church Dogmatics* IV/2. Translated by G. W. Bromiley. Edinburgh: T. & T. Clark, 1958.

———. *Church Dogmatics* IV/4. Translated by Geoffrey W. Bromiley. London: T. & T. Clark International, 1981.

Bauckham, Richard. *Jesus and the Eyewitnesses: The Gospels as Eyewitness Testimony.* 2nd ed. Grand Rapids: Eerdmans, 2017.

Beker, J. Christiaan. *Paul the Apostle: The Triumph of God in Life and Thought.* Philadelphia: Fortress, 1980.

Blake, John. "Predictions about the decline of Christianity in America may be premature." CNN, April 9, 2023. https://www.cnn.com/2023/04/08/us/christianity-decline-easter-blake-cec/index.html.

Blake, William. *The Complete Poetry and Prose of William Blake.* Rev. ed. Edited by David V. Erdman; commentary by Harold Bloom. New York: Anchor, 1988.

Book of Common Prayer. The Episcopal Church. New York: Oxford University Press, 1990.

Boyd, Gregory A. *Crucifixion of the Warrior God.* Vol. 1: *The Cruciform Hermeneutic;* Vol. 2: *The Cruciform Thesis.* Minneapolis: Fortress, 2017.

Bretherton, Luke. *Christ and the Common Life: Political Theology and the Case for Democracy.* Grand Rapids: Eerdmans, 2019.

Brett, Mark G. *Locations of God: Political Theology in the Hebrew Bible*. New York: Oxford University Press, 2019.

Budde, Michael L. *Foolishness to Gentiles: Essays on Empire, Nationalism, and Discipleship*. Theopolitical Visions. Eugene, OR: Cascade, 2022.

Busch, Eberhard. *Karl Barth: His Life from Letters and Autobiographical Texts*. Translated by John Bowden. Eugene, OR: Wipf and Stock, 1976.

Campbell, Will D. *Brother to a Dragonfly*. Banner Book Series. Jackson, MS: University of Mississippi Press, 1977.

Chartier, Gary. *Understanding Friendship: On the Moral, Political, and Spiritual Meaning of Love*. Minneapolis: Fortress, 2022.

Christoyannopoulos, Alexandre. *Christian Anarchy: A Political Commentary on the Gospel*. Abridged ed. Exeter: Imprint Academic, 2011.

Claiborne, Shane, and Michael Martin. *Beating Guns: Hope for People Who Are Weary of Violence*. Grand Rapids: Brazos, 2019.

Clapp, Rodney. *Families at the Crossroads: Beyond Traditional and Modern Options*. Downers Grove, IL: InterVarsity, 1993.

———. *Naming Neoliberalism: Exposing the Spirit of Our Age*. Minneapolis: Fortress, 2021.

———. *A Peculiar People: The Church as Culture in a Post-Christian Society*. Downers Grove, IL: InterVarsity, 1996.

Davis, Ellen F. *Opening Israel's Scriptures*. New York: Oxford University Press, 2019.

Dean, Robert J. *For the Life of the World: Jesus Christ and the Church in the Theologies of Dietrich Bonhoeffer and Stanley Hauerwas*. Eugene, OR: Pickwick, 2016.

Denysenko, Nicholas. *This Is the Day that the Lord Has Made: The Liturgical Year in Orthodoxy*. Eugene, OR: Cascade, 2023.

Dyson, Michael Eric. "'God Almighty Has Spoken from Washington, DC': American Society and Christian Faith." In *The Michael Eric Dyson Reader*, 173–191. New York: Basic Civitas, 2004.

Džalto, Davor. *Anarchy and the Kingdom of God: From Eschatology to Orthodox Political Theology and Back*. Orthodox Christianity and Contemporary Thought. New York: Fordham University Press, 2021.

Eller, Vernard. *Christian Anarchy: Jesus' Primacy over the Powers*. Eugene, OR: Wipf and Stock, 1987.

Ellithorpe, Anne-Marie. *Towards Friendship-Shaped Communities: A Practical Theology of Friendship*. Oxford: Wiley Blackwell, 2022.

Ellul, Jacques. "Anarchism and Christianity." *Katallagete* 7, no. 3 (Fall 1980) 14–24. Retrieved without page numbering at https://theanarchistlibrary.org/library/jacques-ellul-anarchism-and-christianity-en.html.

————. *Anarchy and Christianity*. Translated by Geoffrey W. Bromiley. Grand Rapids: Eerdmans, 1991.

————. *In Season, Out of Season: An Introduction to the Thought of Jacques Ellul*. Translated by Lani K. Niles. New York: Harper and Row, 1982.

Fiddes, Paul S. *Seeing the World and Knowing God: Hebrew Wisdom and Christian Doctrine in a Late-Modern Context*. Oxford: Oxford University Press, 2013.

Fleischer, Matthew Curtis. *The Old Testament Case for Nonviolence*. Oklahoma City: Epic Octavius the Triumphant, 2017.

Fowler, James W. *To See the Kingdom: The Theological Vision of H. Richard Niebuhr*. Lanham, MD: University Press of America, 1974.

Frei, Hans W. *The Eclipse of Biblical Narrative: A Study in Eighteenth and Nineteenth Century Hermeneutics*. New Haven, CT: Yale University Press, 1974.

Fretheim, Terence E. *God and World in the Old Testament: A Relational Theology of Creation*. Nashville: Abingdon, 2005.

Gerstle, Gary. *The Rise and Fall of the Neoliberal Order: America and the World in the Free Market Era*. New York: Oxford University Press, 2022.

Gorringe, Timothy J. *Karl Barth: Against Hegemony*. Christian Theology in Context. New York: Oxford University Press, 1999.

Gorski, Philip S., and Samuel L. Perry. *The Flag and the Cross: White Christian Nationalism and the Threat to American Democracy*. New York: Oxford University Press, 2022.

Gregory, Brad S. *The Unintended Reformation: How a Religious Revolution Secularized Society*. Cambridge, MA: The Belknap Press of Harvard University Press, 2012.

Harink, Douglas. *Resurrecting Justice: Reading Romans for the Life of the World*. Downers Grove, IL: IVP Academic, 2020.

Hartmann, Thom. *The Hidden History of Neoliberalism: How Reaganism Gutted America and How to Restore Its Greatness*. New York: Berrett-Koehler, 2022.

Hauerwas, Stanley. "A Story-Formed Community: Reflections on *Watership Down*." In *A Community of Character: Toward a Constructive Christian Social Ethic*, 9–35. Notre Dame, IN: University of Notre Dame Press, 1981.

Hinlicky, Paul R. *Joshua*. Brazos Theological Commentary on the Bible. Grand Rapids: Brazos, 2021.

Horrell, David G. *Ethnicity and Inclusion: Religion, Race, and Whiteness in Constructions of Jewish and Christian Identities*. Grand Rapids: Eerdmans, 2020.

Howard, Evan B. *Deep and Wide: Reflections on Socio-Political Engagement, Monasticism(s), and the Christian Life*. New Monastic Library: Resources for Radical Discipleship. Eugene, OR: Cascade, 2023.

Jennings, Willie James. *Acts*. Belief: A Theological Commentary on the Bible. Louisville, KY: Westminster John Knox, 2017.

Käsemann, Ernst. *Church Conflicts: The Cross, Apocalyptic, and Political Resistance*. Translated by Roy A. Harrisville. Grand Rapids: Baker Academic, 2021.

Kavanagh, Aidan. *On Liturgical Theology*. Collegeville, MN: Liturgical, 1984.

Keener, Craig S. *The Gospel of John: A Commentary*, vol. 2. Grand Rapids: Baker Academic, 2003.

Kipling, Rudyard. "The White Man's Burden: The United States and The Philippine Islands." https://historymatters.gmu.edu/d/5478/.

Kreider, Alan. *The Patient Ferment of the Early Church: The Improbable Rise of Christianity in the Roman Empire*. Grand Rapids: Baker Academic, 2016.

Lafer, Gordon. "Universalism and Particularism in Jewish Law: Making Sense of Political Loyalties." In *Jewish Identity,* edited by David Theo Goldberg and Michael Krausz, 177–211. Philadelphia: Temple University Press, 1993.

Lamb, Michael. *A Commonwealth of Hope: Augustine's Political Thought.* Princeton, NJ: Princeton University Press, 2022.

Levenson, Jon D. *Sinai and Zion: An Entry into the Jewish Bible.* New Voices in Biblical Studies. San Francisco: HarperOne, 1985.

Lind, Millard C. *Yahweh Is a Warrior: The Theology of Warfare in Ancient Israel.* Scottdale, PA: Herald, 1980.

Lindbeck, George A. "Confession and Community: An Israel-like View of the Church." In *The Church in a Postliberal Age,* edited by James J. Buckley, 1–9. Radical Traditions. Grand Rapids: Eerdmans, 2002.

Loftin, Landon, and Max Leyf. *What Barfield Thought: An Introduction to the Work of Owen Barfield.* Eugene, OR: Cascade, 2023.

Lohfink, Gerhard. *Does God Need the Church? Toward a Theology of the People of God.* Translated by Linda M. Maloney. Collegeville, MN: Michael Glazier, 1999.

Lynerd, Benjamin T. *Republican Theology: The Civil Religion of American Evangelicals.* Oxford: Oxford University Press, 2014.

Mahn, Jason A. *Becoming a Christian in Christendom: Radical Discipleship and the Way of the Cross in America's "Christian" Culture.* Minneapolis: Fortress, 2016.

Mannoussakis, John Panteleimon. "The Anarchic Principle of Christian Eschatology in the Eucharistic Tradition of the Eastern Church." *Harvard Theological Review* 100:1 (2007) 29–46. https://www.jstor.org/stable/4125233.

May, Todd. *Friendship in an Age of Economics: Resisting the Forces of Neoliberalism.* Lanham, MD: Lexington, 2012.

Merton, Thomas. *Conjectures of a Guilty Bystander.* Introduction by Thomas Moore. New York: Image, 1966.

Middleton, J. Richard. *A New Heaven and a New Earth: Reclaiming Biblical Eschatology.* Grand Rapids: Baker Academic, 2014.

Miller, Paul D. *The Religion of American Greatness: What's Wrong with Christian Nationalism.* Downers Grove, IL: IVP Academic, 2022.

———. "A Tale of Two Books, One Podcast, and the Contest over Christian Nationalism: Answering Stephen Wolfe's arguments for blood, soil, and sedition." *Christianity Today,* December 20, 2022. https://www.christianitytoday.com/ct/2022/december-web-only/stephen-wolfe-case-christian-nationalism-paul-miller.html.

Mitchell, C. Ben. "The Christian Origins of Hospitals." Bible Mesh. https://biblemesh.com/blog/the-christian-origins-of-hospitals/.

Moore, Brenna. *Kindred Spirits: Friendship and Resistance at the Edges of Modern Catholicism.* Class 200: New Studies in Religion. Chicago: University of Chicago Press, 2021.

Newbigin, Lesslie. *The Gospel in a Pluralist Society.* Grand Rapids: Eerdmans, 1989.

Niebuhr, H. Richard. *The Responsible Self: An Essay in Christian Moral Philosophy.* New York: Harper and Row, 1963.

———. "Responsibility and Christ." In *The Responsible Self: An Essay in Christian Moral Philosophy,* 161–178. New York: Harper and Row, 1963.

O'Donovan, Oliver. *The Desire of the Nations: Rediscovering the Roots of Political Theology.* Cambridge: Cambridge University Press, 1996.

Patterson, David. *Eighteen Words to Sustain a Life: A Jewish Father's Ethical Will.* Eugene, OR: Cascade, 2023.

Pew Research Center. "Modeling the Future of Religion in America." https:www.pewresearch.org/religion/2022/09/13/modeling-the-future-of-religion-in-America/.

Phillips, Elizabeth. *Apocalyptic Theopolitics: Essays and Sermons on Eschatology, Ethics, and Politics.* Theopolitical Visions. Eugene, OR: Cascade, 2022.

Raekstad, Paul, and Sofa Saio Gradin. *Prefigurative Politics: Building Tomorrow Today.* Cambridge: Polity, 2020.

Rosa, Hartmut. *Resonance: A Sociology of Our Relationship to the World.* Translated by James C. Wagner. Cambridge: Polity, 2019.

———. *The Uncontrollability of the World.* Translated by James C. Wagner. Cambridge: Polity, 2020.

Sanneh, Kelefa. "How Christian Is Christian Nationalism? Many Americans who advocate it have little interest in religion and an aversion to American culture as it currently exists. What really defines the movement?" *New Yorker,* March 27, 2023. https://www.newyorker.com/magazine/2023/04/03/how-christian-is-christian-nationalism.

Scott, James C. *Two Cheers for Anarchism: Six Easy Pieces on Autonomy, Dignity, and Meaningful Work and Play.* Princeton, NJ: Princeton University Press, 2012.

Sharlet, Jeff. *The Undertow: Scenes from a Slow Civil War.* New York: W. W. Norton, 2023.

Soelle, Dorothee. *The Silent Cry: Mysticism and Resistance.* Translated by Barbara and Martin Rumscheidt. Minneapolis: Fortress, 2001.

Taylor, Charles. *A Secular Age.* Cambridge, MA: The Belknap Press of Harvard University Press, 2007.

Thompson, James W. *Christ and Culture in the New Testament.* Eugene, OR: Cascade, 2023.

Tietz, Christiane. *Karl Barth: A Life in Conflict.* Translated by Victoria J. Barnett. Oxford: Oxford University Press, 2021.

Vallier, Kevin. *All the Kingdoms of the World: On Radical Religious Alternatives to Liberalism.* New York: Oxford University Press, 2023.

Van Engen, Abram C. *City on a Hill: A History of American Exceptionalism.* New Haven, CT: Yale University Press, 2020.

Wadell, Paul J. *Friendship and the Moral Life.* Notre Dame, IN: University of Notre Dame Press, 1989.

Wainwright, Geoffrey. *Doxology: The Praise of God in Worship, Doctrine and Life.* A Systematic Theology. New York: Oxford University Press, 1980.

———. *Eucharist and Eschatology.* Akron, OH: OSL, 2002.

Werntz, Myles. *From Isolation to Community: A Renewed Vision for Christian Life Together.* Grand Rapids: Baker Academic, 2022.

Whitehead, Andrew L., and Samuel L. Perry. *Taking America Back for God: Christian Nationalism in the United States.* New York: Oxford University Press, 2020.

Williams, Rowan. *Faith in the Public Square.* London: Continuum, 2012.

———. "Postmodern Theology and the Judgement of the World." In *Theology after Liberalism: A Reader,* edited by John Webster and George P. Schner, 321–332. Oxford: Blackwell, 2000.

Winn, Christian T. Collins. *Jesus, Jubilee, and the Politics of God's Reign.* Prophetic Christianity. Grand Rapids: Eerdmans, 2023.

Wirzba, Norman. *This Sacred Life: Humanity's Place in a Wounded World.* Cambridge: Cambridge University Press, 2021.

Wolfe, Stephen. *The Case for Christian Nationalism.* Moscow, ID: Canon, 2022.

Yong, Amos. *In the Days of Caesar: Pentecostalism and Political Theology.* Sacra Doctrina: Theology for a Postmodern Age. Grand Rapids: Eerdmans, 2010.

Index

Thompson, James, 38n20
Trump, Donald, 52

Van Engen, Abram, 8

Wadell, Paul, 103, 104
Wainwright, Geoffrey, 90, 98,
    99–100
Warren, Tish Harrison, 58n7
Werntz, Myles, 15n8
Williams, Rowan, 47–48, 66n22
Winn, Christian Collins, 30, 89, 93

Winthrop, John, 8
Wirzba, Norman, 15n7, 116–17
Wolfe, Stephen, and *The Case
    for Christian Nationalism,*
    52–66
worship, and duration, 87–88;
    Eucharist, 97–100, 113–14;
    preaching, 90–92, 93–95,
    96–97; as prayer, 123–24; as
    public and political, 88–89

Yong, Amos, 32, 34